DIVORCE - KNOW THE SCORE

Understand the divorce process

and

how to take care of your emotions

GW00391590

ISBN 978-1-8384380-0-5

Copyright © 2021 by

Margaret Yates and Farzana Naz

All rights reserved.

1

INTRODUCTION

No two divorces are the same. However, there are some common questions that Farzana and Margaret have found during the course of their work that are regularly asked by their clients. The purpose of this book is to provide guidance on those questions if you are thinking of separating or getting divorced so that you can get to grips with the process early on.

It will give you an insight as to what to expect during a divorce and how to deal with the emotional side of things. Knowing what to expect in the legal process and how to work through some of the emotional challenges you may face will help relieve some of the stress. The law referred to in this book is the Law of England and Wales. The law does change from time to time. You can check out the current divorce procedure on www.gov.uk and searching "divorce".

You should consider obtaining guidance from a divorce coach or legal advice from a family solicitor before you start your divorce. Every divorce is different, and this book should only be considered as general guidance in terms of the legal aspects. You are strongly advised to seek legal advice before you take any of the legal steps.

In this book you will learn how to:

- Understand the divorce process, financial arrangements and arrangements for children.
- Come to terms with your situation so you can work through it on an informed level.
- Take care of yourself.
- Let go of things you have no control over.
- Reduce your stress levels to give you the clarity you need to make informed and effective decision.
- Understand what is important to you so that you can build a better future.
- Keep strong and focused even in the tough times.
- Emerge from divorce feeling the future is bright.

CONTENTS

CHAPTER 1

IS THIS REALLY THE END OF YOUR RELATIONSHIP?

Ending a marriage can be tough and the longer you were married the more distressing it can be.

The decision to end a marriage isn't one that most people take lightly, and once the roller coaster has started, it's likely to be a wild ride right to the end, whether you are divorcing your spouse or vice versa.

It's a radical step and before taking it, it's worth making the time to check in with yourself that it's the right step for you. (Unless, of course, you are in physical danger and need to take immediate action to keep yourself safe).

So, before you take that first step – Is this really the end of your relationship?

When emotions are running high, it is very difficult to make rational decisions. You are unable to think clearly and may say things that you later come to regret (although at the time you don't think you will!). I have experienced this myself. And I know I speak from the heart when I say that I wish I had taken a step back and retreated to reconsider my response.

If you are stuck in an angry conversation, you know that no matter what you say, you aren't going to change the other person's viewpoint. You can't control what they think or say. You can control your response though.

I've read so many narratives where we are told we should think about how we respond and a list of bullet points to go through. Whilst it's good advice, it's not always easy to do that when you are in the full flow of an emotional argument. When we are getting a full force attack from the other side and are feeling angry and vulnerable ourselves.

However, when an argument starts escalating, it's unlikely to stop until one of you decides to stop playing the game. You can be that person. And that is not giving in or backing down. It's deciding that you've had enough of something that is causing you a tremendous amount of stress and isn't going to get anywhere anyway. There will be no good outcome.

You can stop the conversation by saying something like you need to take a break to think things through and then walk away from the person you are having the argument with, whether that's physically or ending a text session.

This will allow you breathing space and an opportunity to calm down and think more rationally about what the argument was about. You can then decide how you can respond more constructively. Remember, you can only control how you respond. And if the other person is on a different wavelength to you, then it's possible you won't get them to agree to your point of view in any case. Talking things through with someone you trust can help you get a better perspective on what's going on.

Perhaps you've found out your spouse has been having an affair. You may be reeling from the shock and feeling agitated, confused and depressed. These feelings are normal, and you'll probably feel like you're on an emotional roller coaster for a while. It will take time to come to terms with the pain. Sharing the gory details with your children is unfair and will cause them anxiety. Talk things through with a trusted friend or counsellor, who can help you work through your feelings. Take it one day at a time and as you work it through, it will become clearer how to move forward.

It's normal for marriages to go through good times and bad times. But if there are more bad times than good, and you either find yourselves arguing and bickering most of the time or simply indifferent to each other, it may be the case that things aren't going to improve. Very often, people stay in a relationship for months or even years after it has, to all intents and purposes, 'ended'.

Sometimes the demands placed by children and spouses, parents and friends can become over whelming, especially when too much is demanded of our time, or when our relationships change. Fin ancial issues are commonplace for many people. The strain of managing the bills and cost of living, workplace demands, fear of losing their job and as I'm writing this in 2020, the fear of Covid19 and what implications that represents for the future can add to their fears and worries.

I know several people who discovered during lockdown that their marriage wasn't working and have decided to end their relationship. I know others who found that lockdown brought them together and has helped their relationship grow from strength to strength.

Everyone is unique so don't compare yourself with others. Just because your friend is "getting on with it" and staying in their marriage with gritted teeth, doesn't mean you have to. And just because you other friend has had a very difficult experience of divorce, doesn't mean you will. It's your life and there is one thing that you can say with certainty and that is you aren't going to live forever. So, it's definitely worth taking stock just now and checking in with where you are at.

Take some time to consider what's going on in your life right now and whether in fact your marriage is at an end or whether it could be viable with some work done on it.

Here are some things that you might want to consider:

Talk things through with your partner

Can you talk to your partner about the problems in your relationship or does that trigger more arguments?   If you are worried about arguments, perhaps relationship counselling or couple therapy may be a way forward.

Relationship Counselling can help get your relationship back on track

Relationship counselling usually consists of between 1-3 sessions and can help couples recognise and manage their differences. It focusses on the present and the challenges of married life so you can get your relationship back on track.

Relationship counselling aims to

- Provide a confidential, non-judgmental space for you both to hold a constructive dialogue.
- It permits you and your partner to speak freely and have the opportunity of listening to one another.
- It aims to improve communication between you and empowers you both to take charge of your relationship.

Couple Therapy can help with deep rooted problems

Like Relationship Counselling, Couple therapy deals with the present day, but also any history of deep-rooted problem that may be causing unhealthy relationship patterns. Couple therapy usually consists of between 12- 24 sessions.

The Couple therapist will help you to

- Identify the reasons behind the emotions that are driving the unhealthy relationship patterns.
- Communications and how to resolve conflict.
- It can also cover issues such as substance abuse, infidelity and child rearing conflicts.

More details can be found at website www.relate.org.uk www.-counselling-directory.org.uk

Speak to someone you like, know and trust

Do you have a trusted friend who is non-judgmental, won't take sides and could act as a mediator for either or both of you? If they can't act as mentor, would they agree to support you? Having someone you trust to talk things through with can help you get a better perception on what it is happening. It can also help you to view your situation more objectively and be better placed to make the right decisions for you going forward.

Make an appointment with a Divorce Coach

A divorce coach is like any other coach. If you want to play sport better, you need a good coach to show you technique, how to handle yourself and push you to be your best.

A divorce coach does the same thing. They give you guidance on how to handle challenges, techniques on how to communicate with your solicitor and how to have clear strategies so you are thinking 2 or 3 steps ahead of where you are now. Your coach will be objective and give you balanced ideas and suggestions to keep you levelheaded as you progress.

A divorce coach can offer you a safe, confidential space where you can talk through your fears and concerns about your marriage and the future. You'll usually have between 1 - 6 hourly sessions and they can help you to:

- Understand your feelings and emotions and help you look at ways can do to manage them, so you don't feel so stressed and overwhelmed.
- Help you look at practical solutions regarding your financial and housing needs.
- Go through the divorce process with you so that you know what you might expect if you choose to take that route.
- Help you with your paperwork.

You may be thinking why do I need a divorce coach if I already have a solicitor? Surely, I'll be paying double in that case? I understand that you may think that. However, while a divorce coach is another cost, in the long run they will help you keep your legal costs down and save you money in the long run. This is because you won't need to go to your solicitor with every question you have and be billed out at their hourly rate.

This is why I work with family solicitors who understand that it is cost effective to use a divorce coach as part of their team.

Get perspective

Getting perspective of what's going on in your marriage at the moment is important to help you towards your decision about divorce.

Here's an exercise to help you to do that.

EXERCISE 1

7 Questions to help you decide if divorce is the right step for you.

Find a space where you can be comfortable and undisturbed for a spell, take your coffee, a glass of water and your notebook and pen (as you'll want to make notes and jot down answers), and work through the following questions.

1. Why did you get married in the first place?

Some people choose marriage to get out of a situation they're in at the time, rather than getting to know and love their new partner.

- Was it because you were lonely?
- Was it because you were unhappy with your then current circumstances?
- Did you think you'd make the best of it and grow to love them anyway?
- Did you believe you could cure them of those "irritating habits"?
- Did you believe you genuinely loved them?

List 5 reasons why you decided to get married.
(You may want to add more when you really start to think about this – list them all).

I decided to get married because:
1.
2.
3.
4.
5.

Now rate yourself for the first question: On a scale of 1-10 (1 being definitely leave and 10 being definitely stay) where are you on the scale for Q1?

2. What is happening in your marriage that makes you want to divorce?

Is there a way to resolve this? Or is your marriage unable to be saved?

Make a list of all the negative things that you feel that are happening for you. List every single one – no holding back. Get them all out. Now, go back through the list and check:

- How many of those things are about the behaviour of your partner?
- How many of those things are about your behaviour?
- How many of those things do you blame him for?
- How many of those things do you blame yourself for?
- How could you change the way you react in these situations to improve your relationship?

Now list all the positive things that you feel are happening for you and follow the same process as you did for the negative things.

Now rate yourself: On a scale of 1-10 (1 being definitely leave and 10 being definitely stay) where are you on the scale for Q2?

3. Have you threatened to divorce in the past and not followed it through?

In a heated marital argument, it's quite likely that divorce raises its head from time to time. And where divorce is consistently threatened, both parties lose credibility. Was it out of anger or frustration?

- Was it to get them to take you seriously?
- Was it to get them to see things your way?
- Do you genuinely want a divorce to close a chapter on this stage of your life because there is nothing more you can put into this relationship?

Now rate yourself: On a scale of 1-10 (1 being definitely leave and 10 being definitely stay) where are you on the scale for Q4?

4. What is your role in the situation you're in?

No matter how difficult our partner is, we contribute in some way to the problems we're facing. This is not an easy question but take some time over it as it will help you enormously if you understand that you and only you are responsible for your own actions.

This doesn't mean you should blame yourself or feel guilty in any way. Working out why you respond in a particular way can really help you understand what's going on within you. When you understand why you are reacting in a particular way, you can do something about it.

An example might be if your values are conflicting with your spouse. My ex liked to drink himself silly every night and I hated that. I liked a drink, but not on the scale that he did. I used to really worry about him drinking so much because he relied on his car for work and a lot of the time he would be over the drink/drive limit the next day. So, I started to drink some of the wine he brought home each evening in the hope that if I drunk it, he would drink less. This didn't work of course, because he then brought home more wine! So, we were conflicted. And this sometimes made me provocative and angry towards him because his drinking worried me, and I couldn't stop him from drinking excess. I didn't understand his constant need for alcohol.

- Have there been occasions when you've been provocative?
- Have you been unwilling to speak about something that is bothering you and it has subsequently blown up out of all proportion?
- Have you blamed your spouse for how you feel about their behaviour or what they've said?
- Was your relationship good at the start? If it was, and wasn't on shaky ground to start with, at what stage did the problems start? Was there a particular event or situation?

- Have you stayed in a toxic relationship because you felt you should, and you didn't think there was a way out?

Now rate yourself: On a scale of 1-10 (1 being definitely leave and 10 being definitely stay), where are you on the scale for Q3?

5. How would you feel if the next 3 years were like the last 3?

Is getting a divorce now a decision, you may regret, or will it be breaking a long chapter of misery?

Find a comfortable place to sit with a straight back, either in a chair or on a cushion. Rest your hands palms down on your thighs. Make sure your feet at firmly on the floor. As you close your eyes, imagine your feet growing roots, beautiful strong roots that connect right to the centre of the earth.

Follow your breath, slowly and gently, filling your belly and up through to your chest, feel it rise and fall and I want you to imagine that you can take yourself off into your future life 3 years from today. You are still married to your spouse.

- What will you see?
- What will you feel?
- What will you hear people around you say?
- What will you be doing?
- How will you be behaving?

Spend some time doing this and really get into the future.
Now, stand up and clap your hands to break the state.
Sit down again and close your eyes. This time imagine taking yourself into your future 3 years from today. You are no longer with your spouse.

- What will you see?
- What will you feel?
- What will you hear people around you say?
- What will you be doing?
- How will you be behaving?

Again, be prepared to spend some time doing this and really get into it. What could your life look like? Who could you be if you were no longer married?

Which is the future you're going to choose?

Now rate yourself: On a scale of 1-10 (1 being definitely leave and 10 being definitely stay) where are you on the scale for Q5?

6. Are you willing to face up to the challenges ahead confidently and if you decide to divorce?

How you deal with ending the marriage will determine your future. You can decide on revenge, bitterness and aggression or you can negotiate for your future from a position of strength and respect.

Depending on your circumstances it can take anything up to 12 months and sometimes longer to end a marriage and resolve the finances. What can you do to ensure you keep your spirits up and don't get bogged down in the "he said/she said" during this time?

- Are you willing to reach agreements that are good for everyone, not just good for you?
- Are you willing to respect your spouse's rights as well as your own?
- Do you accept that your lifestyle and finances will change?
- Are you willing to let go of your spouse?
- Are you willing to plan for the future rather than staying stuck in the past?

Now rate yourself: On a scale of 1-10 (1 being definitely leave and 10 being definitely stay) where are you on the scale for Question 6.

7. What would have to happen for you to stay in the marriage?

You didn't get married to get divorced and no doubt anticipated that you would be spending the rest of your life with your partner.

Are there any changes that could be made by both of you to get the marriage back on track?

- What would your partner have to do?
- What would you have to do?
- Is there a middle ground?
- Would you be willing to talk things though with your partner either alone or with a mediator?
- Would your partner be willing to talk things through with you either alone or with a mediator?

Now rate yourself: On a scale of 1-10 (1 being definitely leave and 10 being definitely stay) where are you on the scale for Question 7.

Now have a look through your notes and check your ratings. Are most of your answers nearer a 1 than a 10? Do you have a definite "leave", a definite "stay" or are you somewhere in the middle? Chapter 2 will help you if you are still undecided.

SHOULD I STAY OR SHOULD I GO?

*"Inaction and indecision in the present is because of
fear of consequences of the future".*
L.Ron Hubbard

So, now you've got your thoughts out of your head and on to the paper. Have you reached any conclusions?

Have you decided whether you should stay and work at your marriage or leave it?

Are you still in limbo?

Divorce, remain or not sure?

If, after going through the questions, your decision is to divorce or to remain and work on your marriage, you will have made that decision on an informed basis, rather than an emotional one.

You will feel in control of the situation which will help you feel more confident and, in a position, to make the best choices going forward.

Initially, you may feel very scared and worried about the outcome, but often it's much easier to deal with if you come from a decision-based mindset. Once you make a decision, your brain has something tangible to work with and it will look for ways to create that scenario.

But what if you're still feeling unsure as to whether divorce is the right step for you? That's ok. You will know when the time is right what action you need to take. I'll go into this more further on in this chapter.

Divorce

My ex was a binge drinker and when he was under the influence of drink, he could be very challenging. I felt I was between a rock and a hard place. It was like walking on eggshells. I was always worried what state he would come home in, whether he'd be driving under the influence of alcohol and give me third degree inquisition of my movements during the day.

Our friends dwindled away because of his behaviour towards them. I loved to have social gatherings, but he would get drunk and start arguments with people. We never had enough money. I got to the point when I lost weight, became very depressed.

We had planned to emigrate to New Zealand. We didn't know anyone there, but we had done some research and visited New Zealand House in London and started the process. It was an exciting prospect for a while.

But the more I thought about it, the more apprehensive I became. In those days you could opt for a family passport, which was much cheaper than us all having our own passports.

I felt that once I arrived in New Zealand, I would have no one to turn to if things didn't work out. Also, I would be pretty much trapped there and unable to return to the UK, as I didn't have my own passport. I couldn't afford to buy my own and if I did, I certainly wouldn't have wanted to leave my children behind.

I agonised for months over whether I should go to New Zealand with my husband. I really did not want to stop him, but I didn't want to go with him whilst he remained a binge drinker.

I could not see the way forward - how could I manage on my own with 3 children to care for? I was working part time at a local hospital at the time and I couldn't possibly pay the mortgage myself, what would I do for money? Was it my fault? Was it really as bad as I thought it was? Was it just me? How would my husband react when I told him I wasn't coming to New Zealand with him? On the other hand, a future living with him filled me with dread. I felt as if my head would burst at times.

I had no one that I could talk through my problems with at the time. Family members were far away, and I had no friends to turn to anymore. There were no divorce coaches in those days and Relate was then known as the Marriage Guidance service which at that time was more towards mending the marriage than helping peaceful separation. I think I knew at that point I didn't want to save my marriage; it was too late. He was never going to stop drinking and I really couldn't cope with the stress and behaviour that accompanied that. But I didn't know how to get out of it.

At the time, I was working as secretary to a chest consultant, Dr Anderson, at Cheddon Road Hospital. He helped my mother when she was suffering from lung cancer. He was very precise and particular in the way he liked things done. He'd do a bronchoscopy and pop back into the office to dictate his notes before moving on to the next patient. (I used to smoke at the time and after typing up an account of someone's lungs being destroyed by smoking, I'd still go outside for a cigarette. That's how stressed I was!).

Dr Anderson was a very caring individual and I ended up talking to him about my concerns. I just didn't know whether to carry on with the New Zealand plan or not. He was very kind and a good listener. He told me to trust my instinct to know what to do when the time was right.

One morning, I can remember it well, something broke inside of me. I had had enough. I was very nervous, but I knew I had to do it. I told my husband that I wasn't going to come to New Zealand with him unless he gave up drinking. I told him I just couldn't cope with his drinking. I knew, when he came home at lunchtime smelling of alcohol that it wasn't going to make any difference what I said. He would still continue to drink. At that point I realised I had to get out. I told him that if he couldn't stay off the drink for a morning, then I wanted a divorce.

He just laughed in my face. Called me some unspeakable names and went back to work. I was very scared of what he might do, but I couldn't take any more. I knew he wouldn't hurt the children other than speak to them about me unkindly, which of course he did. He eventually got the message when he received my solicitor's letter. I had to put up with a lot of abusive insults and to cut a long and very intense story short, he eventually left.

If you are scared of leaving because of what your spouse might do, please talk things through with someone first and make a proper plan. Don't leave it all to chance as I did.

One of the things I should have thought about was where I could go if he did turn on the children and me. Luckily, I didn't need to, but it could have been very different.

I had no idea what to do next after I had told him I wanted a divorce, other than find a solicitor. In hindsight, I wish I had got legal advice before I told him I wanted a divorce. That way I would have understood what I might be entitled to. As it was, my husband span all sorts of stories and myths about what would happen to the children and I. It caused me a huge amount of unnecessary stress that I could have avoided, had I done my homework properly in the beginning.

Remain in the marriage

If you decided you would like to remain in the marriage, what can you do to get it back on track? What changes did you decide you would you like to see in the marriage? What changes would you be prepared to make?

I remember one of my clients, (I'll call her Yvette to keep confidentiality) came to me because she believed she wanted divorce. She felt she was drifting along in a loveless, unhappy marriage. She had been married for 30 years. Sex life had never been great but had now become non-existent and her husband behaved as if she wasn't there. He didn't take much interest in her, preferring to work and play golf rather than take time out with her. He'd never been one for 'date nights' and did not like much fuss.

He provided for his family and it seems felt like that was his role in life. This worked whilst she had the children as she took an active part in their lives and pretty much ran the home single handed. Over the years, Yvette had taken most major decisions in the running of the household. However, now the children had left home, life was looking pretty bleak.

Whenever Yvette wanted anything done, there would always be an argument. She found it very tiring and when she did talk with her husband and asked for his input into for example where to go on holiday, he'd always reacted by arguing why they shouldn't go, but then give in and agree. Yvette said it was so predictable that he wasn't going to agree with her and usually gave up early on in most arguments. As we talked, I found out that this had been going on since they got married. It was nothing new. He would argue his point and then agree. It was as if he had to put his point across first before agreeing the outcome.

In fact, none of what Yvette was telling me was new. She was just focusing more on it now because she had so much time on her hands now the children had left home. She was beginning to wonder "Is this all my life is about?

So why did she think he would he change now? He was simply behaving as he always behaved. It was Yvette who now felt she had had enough.

We looked at his behaviour and ways she could reframe her approach and focus on the outcome she wanted. By doing this, it would take away the resentment and anger that she felt towards her husband. Changing her approach could also change his reaction too.

We also talked about her feelings now the children had left home. Her husband still had his work and golf, but she was feeling redundant and not wanted any more. We talked about things she liked to do before she got married and it turned out that she had given up a nursing career. We explored whether this might be something she could go back to and this got her thinking about how she might do that.

It also transpired that Yvette had never asked her husband to sit down and talk about things that were bothering her. She assumed that he wasn't interested so she didn't bother.

Yvette left saying she would take the new approach with her husband. She wanted to go on holiday. Rather than get annoyed, she'd accept that he would bluster about it initially but that he would eventually agree. She would also make an opportunity to talk to her husband about how she felt and if it didn't work out, she would come back and talk more about divorce.

Yvette didn't come back. I saw her three months later. She had been on a wonderful holiday to a spa with a golf course attached. Her husband loved the golf, and she loved the spa! They had taken an opportunity to talk things through and other surprise he was happy that she was thinking about re-training. They had also agreed to have a date night once a week.

So, in Yvette's case, it was worth stopping and thinking about what was actually going on in the marriage and whether there was anything she could do about it, rather than jumping straight into divorce.

Not sure

If you are still in limbo, living with indecision can be much tougher than making a decision. And the longer you live with it, the more likely it is to take its toll on your health, your work and your life in general. You've probably talked your situation through again and again with your friends and perhaps you've even spoken to your family too. They've all given you their opinion. But still you haven't taken any action.

Indecision is like wanting to drive away in your car with your foot on the accelerator and leaving the handbrake on. We've all done it at some stage! But you quickly realise what's happened, release the handbrake and the car moves forward.

Imagine though if you didn't release the handbrake. You are revving and revving the engine, but not getting anywhere. If you continue revving the car without removing the handbrake, eventually the car will start shaking, the engine will be straining and start to smell of burning metal and eventually burn out. The conflict between moving and not moving.

Not making a decision means that thoughts are constantly going around in your head. What happens if I do...? What happens if I don't...? I'm worried that if I do this, that will happen.... or if I don't do this, this will happen......The longer you leave your thoughts in your head the more confused you'll become.

Negative thoughts lead to negative feelings and behaviours. If you are constantly worrying about something, it can cause you to feel stressed, frustrated and irritable. You may be getting angry over things you don't usually get angry about, or perhaps you've been irritable with your children or your best friend. That makes you feel worse because you know that's not you and so you start to feel guilty. You can't think properly, and you can't eat (or perhaps you are eating too much). If you don't do something about it, you may find yourself starting to feel physically ill with headaches and body aches and fatigue.

So, what can you do to get those thoughts in perspective?
Here's an exercise that can help you work out what's worrying you and look at different ways of dealing with your indecision:

EXERCISE 2 – In limbo

Write down everything that is going on in your life right now. Write everything down just as it comes, not in any particular order. Use a pen or pencil rather than an electronic notebook because writing by hand actually increases neural activity in certain sections of the brain - a bit similar to meditation. Why?

When you write things down, it takes them out of your head and onto the paper. This means that you now have control over them. You can see them for what they are. And if you have them under control you can decide what to do with them. When they are in your head, they just keep going round and round. On paper, you bring them into the physical world, and you can look at them and decide which thoughts are useful and which are not. You can then think about how to reframe the thoughts that are not useful.

Writing about anger, sadness and other painful emotions will help to release the intensity of those feelings and you will feel calmer. Writing things down will help you know what you do want and what makes you feel happy and confident.

You'll become clearer about situations and people who are toxic for you, which is important for your emotional wellbeing.

Writing about misunderstandings and disagreements, rather than keeping the anger going can help you understand what's going on for you and you may come up with a resolution to what's bothering you.

The following exercise can help you work out your decision.

EXERCISE 3 – Decision Making

Decision Making

IF I DO..   IF I DON'T....................................

What WOULD happen if I DID make the change? (1)	What WOULD happen if I DIDN'T make the change? (3)
What WOULDN'T happen if I DID make this change? (2)	What WOULDN'T happen if I DIDN'T make this change? (4)

Consequences

How to use the grid
- Write your goal/outcome on the line above the quadrants. *"If I do [write your outcome here] and If I don't [write your outcome here]".*

- Answer the questions in the order 1-4 starting top left. The questions may seem strange or repetitive and that's ok. Focus on what would happen for you and also what would happen to people around you. This is not to cause guilt, but simply to help you to understand the consequences and the outcomes for you and those around you and what you need to think about going forward. A planning trip rather than a guilt trip!

- Allow plenty of time to really think and feel each question, especially question 4 which can confuse your conscious mind! Use separate sheets of paper if you need more space. You might like to use a sheet for each question.

- When you think you've finished answering each question, arrange your 4 pieces of paper (if you used them) in line with the quadrant so that you can see your answers. Then I want you to take a moment to dig deeper and ask yourself "What else?"

- Don't worry if you don't have the answers right away. Sometimes it may be a few hours or even a day or so before the answer "kick's in".

CHAPTER 3

NOW YOU'VE DECIDED

"A journey of a thousand miles begins with a single step".
Lao Tzu

So now you've done the exercises in the exercise book relating to Chapters 1 and 2 and you've decided either to stay and make your marriage work or enough is enough and it's time to leave.

Whichever decision you have reached, there is work to be done.

Stay and Make it Work

"If you always do what you've always done, you'll always get what you always got" said Henry Ford

It's no good just deciding to stay and hope that things will work out. You need to have a plan and a purpose. As the saying goes, if what you were doing didn't work, if you keep doing it, it still won't work.

So, what changes will you need to make to help get things back on track?

EXERCISE 4 - Stay and Make it Work

Are any of the following statements true for you?

- We are like ships that pass in the night. We don't spend time with each other anymore.
- My spouse only pays attention to me when he/she wants sex.
- We haven't been out on a date in years
- My spouse doesn't care about anyone but themselves.
- We're always rowing.
- I feel I'm alone in this marriage.
- My spouse is no longer my friend.

You may have answered "yes" to some or all of them.

Is this why you feel divorce is the only way forward, but you just can't make up your mind?

What if these statements read:

- We make sure we schedule time to be together
- We both pay attention to each other's needs
- We regularly go out on date nights
- We both care about how the other feels
- We have arguments but we work them out together
- I feel part of this marriage
- My spouse is my friend as well as my lover

What would need to change?

Answer the questions that were relevant to you:

- Why are you not spending quality time together? What's getting in the way?
- Why does your spouse only pay attention to you when they want sex? What is stopping them paying attention to you at other times?
- Why don't you go out on date nights? Have you arranged one only to be let down? What's going on here?
- Why do you think your spouse only cares about himself? Is this really true? Does he never do anything for you anymore?
- What are you always rowing about? Is there something you can do about it?
- Why do you feel alone in the marriage? What does that look like to you?
- What is it that makes you believe your spouse is no longer your friend?

EXERCISE 4 - Stay

What Behaviours Need to Change?

Behaviour	Change

What behaviours need to change? Use this grid to work out what needs to change.

Leave

If you've decided that you have had enough and want to leave, you'll need to think about the practicalities for yourself and your children (if you have young children still at home). You'll also need to think about the emotions that you may encounter along the way.

Just because you have made the decision to leave doesn't mean that you won't feel sad, unhappy or guilty about that decision from time to time. It's natural to feel these feelings as you will be experiencing a loss, the loss of your marriage, the loss of your hopes and dreams for the future.

You may find yourself in tears for no particular reason. Being aware that these feelings may arise and knowing that they are a natural way to process a loss can help you understand that it's ok to feel them and that they will pass eventually.

You'll need to get your support team together. Going through divorce can be stressful and challenging and if you have the right support team, they'll help you get through it when the going gets tough and your soon to be ex throws a spanner in the works.

A good support team can include:

- Divorce coach
- Trusted family members or friends that you can call any time
- Family solicitor
- Financial adviser

It's worth making an appointment with a divorce coach so that you know that you have someone who will listen and help look after your emotional needs and the practicalities of leaving your marriage.

A family solicitor can help you to check what your position is with regard to the financial aspects of the marriage. You can then be clearer on what your starting position is what is likely to be the division of the assets.

Once you know your likely position, you may need to have a meeting with a financial adviser who can help you work out what funds you might need and what your mortgage capacity might be with regard to housing. They can give you advice on pension sharing.

Knowing this information at the beginning can help you to be more focused on how you are going to cope at the end of the marriage. If it seems dire to start with, that can be a worry. No one wins in a divorce and both parties are likely to have to take a drop in their standard of living. But remember, this is the start, it's not the end. This is why it is so important for you to have a plan and a purpose.

EXERCISE 5 - Leave

Divorce Support Team

My Divorce Support Team	
Divorce Coach	Solicitor
Financial Adviser	Friends
Family Members	Anyone else?

Think about who you could have in your support team, so that you have someone to call on when the going gets tough and complete their details in the grid above.

EXERCISE 6 - Divorce Concerns

In the next table, think about the things that concern you most

Divorce Concerns		
I am concerned about...	How can I work through it?	What help might I need?

about divorce and write them down in the first column.   In the second column, think about what you can do to work through it. And in the third column list any support you need.

For example: The biggest worry for most people is where they are going to live. So, in the My Concerns column, you'll write 'Where will I live after divorce'.

If you aren't sure about that, think about what you need to know so that you will have an idea of where you might live. For example, it will help you to know what share of the financial assets you may be entitled to. Once you have an idea of what finances are available to you, you can make plans. So, in the second column you can write, for example, 'I need to know my financial options'.

So, who can help you work out your financial options? A divorce coach or family solicitor can help you work out what your legal entitlement might be. So, in the support column you can write 'divorce coach/family solicitor'.

Now think about all the worries and concerns you have and write them down in the first column. You may not be able to think about how to work through them all to start with, and that's ok. By talking to a trusted friend or adviser, you'll be able to put things in place so that you approach your divorce on an informed basis and will not be so fearful about the unknown.

CHAPTER 4

CAN I DIVORCE AND
IS DIVORCE THE ONLY OPTION?

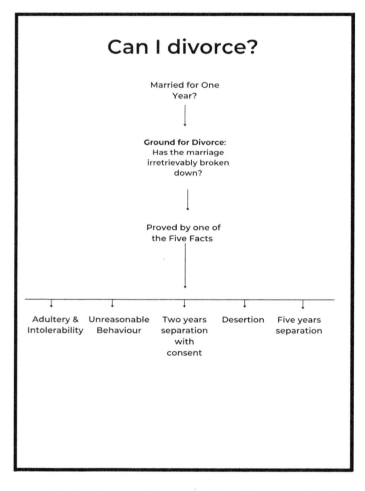

The current legislation requires you to have been married for one year before you can start divorce proceedings, says Farzana.

When considering whether you should go down the route of divorce you should bear in mind that divorce is not the only option available.

There are options such as annulment and judicial separation. However, you would need to meet the requirements to apply for either one of them.

Some people do not want a divorce due to religious reasons and therefore judicial separation may be a better option. The procedure to apply for an annulment or judicial separation is similar to a divorce. However, if you are judicially separated and wish to marry in the future then you will firstly need to obtain a divorce. This is why many prefer to go down the route of divorce. It is best to get it over and done with.

Annulment will void or make a marriage voidable. However, unlike a divorce you do not need to be married for a year to apply to annul the marriage. I have dealt with a number of cases where I have assisted spouses to annul their marriage. Some spouses stated that they realised that they had made a mistake, marriage was never consummated, or they were forced into the marriage. There have been cases where couples have been married for a couple of days and then applied for an annulment.

I recall assisting a wife to annul her marriage who had been married for a few days. Her husband was a lot older than her. They had met abroad whilst on holiday and decided to get married. However, the wife soon after realised that she had made a mistake. She discovered that her husband had a problem with snoring so on the wedding night she slept in a separate bedroom. A few days later she found out that her husband was also in touch with his ex.

Throughout the annulment proceedings the husband pleaded for the wife to reconcile with him as it did not want the marriage to be annulled. The marriage was annulled although there were many hurdles that came in the way during the process.

There was another case that I dealt with where the wife had been forced to get married by her boyfriend to his friend in order to help him secure leave to remain in the UK. She realised that what she had done was wrong and wanted to annul the marriage. She was worried that she may get into trouble by the authorities due to taking part in the sham marriage but luckily this was prevented.

A solicitor will be able to advise you what would be the best route for you to take and will advise you of the options so that you can then make a decision. The solicitor will also explain what the procedure is and the requirements that you need to meet. It is important that you listen carefully to the advice of the solicitor. There is no point going down a route if you do not meet the requirement.

CHAPTER 5

HOW TO CHOOSE A FAMILY SOLICITOR

If you have never had any contact with any legal professionals, then you may wonder how you should decide, which family solicitor to instruct to help you resolve your matrimonial issues.

You firstly need to think about what issues you want the solicitor to help you with i.e. divorce, financial, children or all three. Some solicitors only specialise in a particular area of law and some only deal with for example divorce matters. You need to check if a solicitor deals with the issues that you need help on. It makes sense to instruct one solicitor who can deal with all the issues.

You should try to find a solicitor who is a member of the Law Society's Family Law Panel as the solicitor would specialise in family law and the panel is a recognised quality standard of family lawyers. You should also locate a solicitor who is a member of Family Resolution. Family solicitors who are members of Resolution will abide by a code of practice and they would deal will matters on non-conflict basis such as myself. I believe going go court should be the last resort and if possible, you should try to resolve matters amicably where possible.

You can check a solicitor's website, which will give you details of the areas of law the firm covers and may give a profile of the solicitor. You can also look up the details of the solicitor on the Law Society's website https://solicitors.lawsociety.org.uk/

Family solicitors have different approaches, and some are more sympathetic and good at listening than others. You may find it helpful to have an initial consultation meeting with the solicitor. This will give you an opportunity to assess and decide if the solicitor is the right person to handle your case for you. You need to be comfortable with the solicitor that you instruct as you will be discussing personal information about yourself.

CHAPTER 6

SORT YOUR STRESS OUT

"You cannot always control what goes on outside. But you can always control what goes on inside."
– Wayne Dyer

Challenges are a part of daily life, says Margaret. Most people experience a rewarding home life. However, at times the demands placed by children, partners, parents and siblings can be overwhelming. Juggling a peaceful home life with outside demands can be trying. Friendships can cause demands on our time, which may cause arguments to arise, and relationships change or end.

Our responses to daily challenges are triggered by our own life experiences.

What can be a negative challenge to one person can be a positive challenge to another. For example, some people may find divorce an opportunity to embrace a new life, whereas others feel that it's the end of their world and find it difficult to cope.

Generally, we can cope with day to day problems, but anything added to that which puts high demands on us or changes that force us to adjust can cause overwhelm.

These situations and pressures cause us to feel stressed and are known as "stressors". Most people consider stressors are negative, however, anything that puts high demands upon us can be stressful. Positive events, like buying a house, having a baby, gaining promotion at work.

Nearly half of all adults feel stressed every day or every few days. If a person is constantly on edge because of excessive stress in their life, they may face serious health problems. This is because the body's 'fight or flight' reaction is constantly switched on.

As I mentioned briefly in Chapter 2, this happened to me. For years I had been constantly on tenterhooks, I wasn't able to relax as I didn't know what my husband would do next.

When I finally decided to divorce him, I was even more scared of what he'd do. He kept changing his mind about where he was going to go. We were supposed to be emigrating New Zealand, but I didn't want to go because we had a family passport, and I was really worried I wouldn't be able to come back to the UK if I couldn't cope. Given his bouts of drunkenness, I didn't want to get stuck in NZ with no one to turn to.

At least I knew people in the UK and knew how the UK worked! I was constantly on edge, I lost weight, and all the time having to care for my children who at the time were aged, 3, 4 and 11. When he finally walked out, my body was finally able to let go of the fear and the 'fight or flight' mode it was in.

I collapsed. I became very ill with a serious throat infection. I couldn't get out of bed and I remember the doctor calling several times. It took me months to get over it. There was no counselling in those days, just the threat of having my children removed from me if I wasn't able to care for them! It was a long, hard journey, and I got through it eventually.

Stress is a natural part of life that helps us cope with day to day challenges. A small amount of stress can help us to deal with things that are going on around us.

Our body is a marvellous machine, and the stress response is the body's way of protecting us. When it's working properly, the stress response helps us to stay focused, energetic and alert. In emergency situations, stress can be a lifesaver - it causes us to jump back onto the pavement if we are in danger of being run over by a bus.

Stress also helps us to meet challenges - it keeps us on our toes at work, drives us to meet deadlines such as completing a study or work assignment. However, beyond a certain point stress stops being useful and starts to cause damage to our health, mood, productivity and quality of life.

If we are constantly on edge because of excessive stress, we may end up with serious health problems. This is because our body's 'fight or flight' mode is constantly switched on.

So, what is the fight or fight mode? You've probably heard of it, but perhaps don't know exactly how it works. It's useful to understand the process because it will help you to know when you start to feel stressed. Knowing what is triggering stress for you can help

How Stress Affects your Body

Primary Stress Response
IMMEDIATE AND URGENT RESPONSE TO A SERIOUS THREAT

HEART: Starts pounding and sends blood around the body carrying sugar for energy and stress hormones adrenaline.

SKIN: pales as blood is diverted to major organs.

MUSCLES: tense in readiness for action.

LUNGS: breathing becomes more intense to provide more oxygen to feed increased blood supply.

SWEAT GLANDS start to cool the underlying and overheated muscles.

BLADDER/RECTUM muscles relax to release any excess load.

BLOOD: thickens to help carry more oxygen stop bleeding and fight infection.,

DIGESTION: processes shut down as blood is diverted elsewhere. Mouth goes dry to avoid adding extra fluid to stomach.

LIVER: glycogen is converted to blood sugar to give short term energy.

you look at ways of dealing with it so as to reduce it.
When we encounter perceived threats, the hypothalamus (a small region at the base of our brain) sets of an alarm system in the body. Through a combination of nerve and hormonal signals, the system prompts the adrenal glands (located on top of the kidneys) to release a surge of hormones, including adrenaline and cortisol.

Adrenaline causes the heart rate to increase, raises blood pressure and boosts energy supplies. Cortisol, the primary stress hormone, increases sugars in the bloodstream, enhances the brains use of glucose and increases the availability of substances that repair tissues.

Cortisol also curbs functions that would be non-essential or detrimental in a fight or flight situation. It alters the immune system's responses and slows down the digestive system, the reproductive system and growth processes. This complex natural alarm sys-

How Stress Affects your Body

Secondary Stress Response

BODY'S RESPONSE TO ONGOING STRESS

HEART: racing heartbeat and high blood pressure can lead to strokes/heart failure.

SKIN: continuing less blood supply can lead to skin disease.

MUSCLES: ongoing tension leads to aches and pains and muscle strain.

LUNGS: over oxygenated blood can lead to fainting spells and upset heart rhythm.

DIGESTION: shutdown can lead to stomach problems. Increased acidity can lead to stomach ulcers.

SWEAT GLANDS start to cool the underlying and overheated muscles.

BLADDER/RECTUM muscles relax to release any excess load.

BLOOD: thickened blood causes the heart to work harder.

LIVER: body's own fats and proteins broken down and released to provide further energy.

tem also communicates with regions of the brain that control mood, motivation and fear.

This fight or flight response is a natural response and usually self-regulates once the perceived threat is past. The body returns to normal as the adrenaline and cortisol levels drop.

However, when you constantly feel stressed, tense and nervous, the fight of flight response stays switched on. The long-term activation of the stress response system and subsequent over expos ure to cortisol and other stress hormones can disrupt how the body functionThis can put you at risk of developing health problems such as being prone to colds and 'flu, heart disease, diabetes, digestive problems, sleep disturbances, worsening skin conditions such as eczema and acne. It can also cause you to feel anxious and may lead to you experiencing panic attacks. It is for these reasons that it is so important to recognise the symptoms of stress early and find healthy ways to cope.

Stress itself isn't an illness, it's our body's response to a perceived threat. There is little we can do to prevent it, but there are many things we can to do manage it effectively and reduce our stress levels.

It's well known that divorce is one of the top major stressful events that anyone can ever experience.

Having your world turned upside down, not knowing where you'll live, whether you'll have enough money, how the children (if you have any) will react, what other people in your life will say, will your friends still keep in touch? What will it be like living on your own? Believing you're too old to find someone else. All these thoughts can keep going round and round in your head - if you let them. What you don't know can cause much greater fear and stress that what you do know.

Planning is key

This is why it is so important to make a plan, ideally before if you are able to, or certainly at the beginning when the divorce process starts. Plans can be updated and amended to allow for changes as the process progresses. But if you don't have a plan, you'll just drift, you won't have anything to focus on for the future, and feel you are at the mercy of others.

If you've tried to resolve your differences with your partner and that hasn't worked, then it's likely the marriage is over. You will fare much better if you can start looking to the future rather than staying stuck in the past.

Moving forward gives you momentum to think about new and different ideas of how you'll cope. You may not think you can do this right now, and probably, on your own, it will be hard. It is much easier if you have someone helping you through this. This is where your support team comes into play.

Self-care

Getting to grips with the practicalities is a great start. You also need to think about self care. What can you do to help alleviate stress and overwhelm and feel more relaxed and able to cope? Here are some ideas. Remember, everyone is different and some things may appeal to you more than others. Finding something that you can feel comfortable doing and that works for you is key.

• Taking regular physical exercise can be very effective in receiving stress. This is because of the endorphins (feel good hormones) that the body releases when exercising. A 30 minute walk is a good start.

• You may find it difficult to relax - how do you do that when you are so worried about everything going on just now? As well as good exercise for the physical body, regular sessions of Yoga, Tai Chi and Qigong can help with calming your emotions and relieving stress.

• Breathing techniques - taking slow deep breaths can help you to feel more relaxed.

• Take some "me" time. Have a massage, pamper yourself, take some time out to do some things that you love doing, whatever makes you happy.

• Getting enough sleep is important. Sleeping problems are common in people who are experiencing stress. There are some very good relaxation apps on the market that you can use to help you relax and sleep. One I use is by Glenn Harrold called "Relax and Sleep Well". There is a free version you can try out. You can find out more about it here: http://www.relaxandsleepwell.com

- If you are really struggling, and finding it difficult to cope, make an appointment with your GP, who should be able to advise about treatment.

- Know your limits. Are there any tasks you can delegate? Prioritise tasks to relieve the feeling that everything needs doing at once. The next exercise "Letting Go" can help you with this.

EXERCISE 7 - Letting Go

Letting Go		
Within my Control	I can Influence	Outside my Control

1. What are the things that are contributing to your feeling of overwhelm? These might be worrying about your future, feeling tired, worrying about your finances, feelings of guilt.

2. Write them all out on a sheet of paper or type them up. Get them all out of your head and onto paper.

3. Then follow the instructions below to add each Overwhelm to your Letting Go Chart:

- If you have **complete control** over the issue or problem, (you can resolve it on your own without needing anyone else's help or input) write it down in the first column "Within My Control'. Then move on to the next issue.

- If you have **partial control** or can **influence** the issue or problem (you can resolve part of it or influence the outcome through your own actions or behaviour) write it down with the second column "I Can Influence". Then move on to the next issue.

- If the issue is **completely out of your control or influence** (there is nothing you can say or do that would have a direct impact) write it down in the third column labeled "Everything Else". Then move on to the next issue.

- Once you have written down all your Overwhelm problems or issues and added them to the appropriate spheres/space, here's what you do next:

- For each of the issues you have **control** overtake **action** on at least one of these **today** (or even **right now**) - you'll feel better instantly.

- For each of the issues or problems you have **partial control or influence** over, write down the steps you will take and when you will do them, together with what else or who else you need to assist you.

- For each of the issues or problems that are completely out or your control or influence, let them go! They have no power over you. If you can't control or influence an issue, you are wasting your energy thinking about it

Focus on the issues you have control or influence over.Let everything else go.

CHAPTER 7

FIRST MEETING WITH A FAMILY SOLICITOR

If it's your first time seeing a solicitor, you may feel nervous or even intimidated. Just remember that the solicitor is on your side and there to help you resolve your problems.

There is no need to feel nervous, anxious or intimidated as the solicitor is only a human being at the end of the day. If you do feel anxious or nervous, take some deep breaths and make sure you have prepared for the meeting.

Write down all the questions you have and make sure you have the paperwork you need (see checklist below). Being properly prepared can help you feel in control of the situation and less anxious.

You can always take someone with you to the meeting although the solicitor will want to hear from you, and you will be expected to provide the solicitor with instructions.

So, what can you do to prepare for the meeting? Well, I have created a checklist of the documents and information that you should take to the first meeting.

It is important that you tell your solicitor the full facts of your case. Do not try to hide anything even if it sounds really bad. If you do not give the full facts, then it could have an impact on your case or the advice your solicitor gives.

There is nothing worse than the other side's solicitor telling your solicitor about something you have not already disclosed to your solicitor.

Usually at the first meeting your solicitor will give you an opportunity to explain your circumstances, the problems you are facing, why you have come to a solicitor and what solution you are seeking. It is best to write down any important dates and incidents in a chronological order before you have the meeting.

A solicitor will usually take some notes. Try to focus on what questions you are being asked by your solicitor and try not to keep repeating the same information. You may be paying for the meeting and it's important you get the most out of it.

Do give your solicitor the chance to advise you and listen to the advice given. Sometimes there is a lot of information that is given but the solicitor will usually confirm the advice in writing. So, there is no need to make notes, just pay attention.

If you do not understand any legal terms or the advice being given just ask the solicitor to repeat it. Ask what options are available to you so that you can decide what you want to do.

A solicitor who is a member of Family Resolution will try and help you resolve matters without involving the courts if possible.

By the end of the first meeting, you will have been provided with some advice. Your legal rights in respect of the dissolution of the marriage will have been explained to you, together with what options are available.

A good solicitor will advise you the best course of action to take. Going to court is not always the best way forward.

Preparing for your first meeting with your Divorce Solicitor
You may feel a bit apprehensive before your first meeting with your divorce solicitor. This is quite natural.

You'll probably be feeling stressed and worried about your relationship break up and not knowing about or understanding what action you can or can't take be daunting.

You may be feeling scared that you'll lose your home, or that there will be difficulties with handling arrangements for the children. Where will you find the income you need?

Remember, your solicitor is there to help you work through the process. You can help your solicitor by making sure you are prepared before each meeting and that you have the relevant paperwork/information to bring with you.

For your first meeting with your divorce solicitor, you'll need to bring with you:

- Details of your full name, postal address, email address and telephone number.

- Details of your spouse's full name, postal address, email address and telephone number if you have it.

- Your Marriage Certificate. If you cannot find it, you can obtain an official copy from https://www.gov.uk/order-copy-birth-death-marriage-certificate.

- The names, dates of birth and school details of all the children in your home, regardless of whether they are from this marriage or not.

- Your employment details and details of earnings. Your P60 will show your annual earnings, so bring this document with you. If you can't find your P60, your last three months' pay slips.

- Your spouse's employment details and earnings. If you have a copy of his P60 or pay slips, that would be helpful, but you may not have these documents.

- Your National Insurance Number.

- Details of all property either owned jointly by you and your spouse or in your sole name, including the date the property was purchased, the purchase price and an estimated current value of the property.

- You can find out values of similar properties in your area at http://www.ourproperty.co.uk/ and http://www.zoopla.co.uk/. If you are unsure who owns the property, if the property is registered, you should be able to find out by obtaining office copies of the title of the property here https://www.gov.uk/topic/land-registration/searches-fees-forms.

- If the property is mortgaged, you'll need to provide details of your lender and a copy of the latest mortgage statement.

- Details of any other assets, including all savings, pensions, stocks and shares

- Details of any debts such as loans, credit and store cards, owed by you, your spouse or jointly with your spouse.

- Details of your financial contributions towards the properties/household.

- A brief summary of the main events that have taken place that have led to the breakdown of the marriage, such as:

  - The date you decided the marriage had broken down and the circumstances of breakdown.

  - If you have already separated, the date of separation. If your spouse has returned during the separation period, provide dates.

  - Where there have been incidents of domestic violence or abuse, the dates and a brief description of the incidents and whether the police have been involved.

  - Details of contact arrangements for the children.

  - Anything else you feel might be useful or relevant.

CHAPTER 8

STEPS IN UNDEFENDED DIVORCE

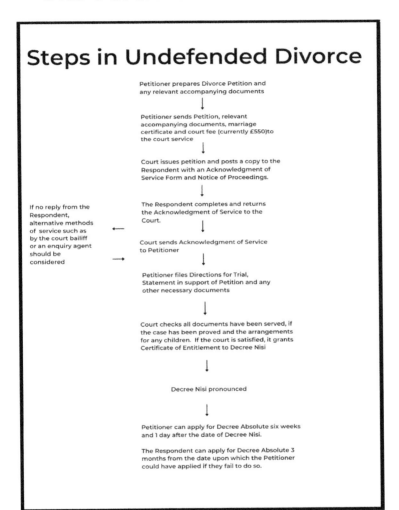

Steps in Undefended Divorce

Petitioner prepares Divorce Petition and any relevant accompanying documents

Petitioner sends Petition, relevant accompanying documents, marriage certificate and court fee (currently £550)to the court service

Court issues petition and posts a copy to the Respondent with an Acknowledgment of Service Form and Notice of Proceedings.

The Respondent completes and returns the Acknowledgment of Service to the Court.

If no reply from the Respondent, alternative methods of service such as by the court bailiff or an enquiry agent should be considered

Court sends Acknowledgment of Service to Petitioner

Petitioner files Directions for Trial, Statement in support of Petition and any other necessary documents

Court checks all documents have been served, if the case has been proved and the arrangements for any children. If the court is satisfied, it grants Certificate of Entitlement to Decree Nisi

Decree Nisi pronounced

Petitioner can apply for Decree Absolute six weeks and 1 day after the date of Decree Nisi.

The Respondent can apply for Decree Absolute 3 months from the date upon which the Petitioner could have applied if they fail to do so.

1. The first step is for the Petitioner to complete the divorce petition. The Petitioner needs to demonstrate that the marriage has irretrievably broken down due to adultery, unreasonable behaviour, desertion, 2 years' separation or 5 years' separation.

2. The Petitioner then sends divorce petition, together with the original marriage certificate and court fee, (which is currently £550). You can check the current court fee here: https://www.gov.uk/court-fees-what-they-are

3. The court will check the petition and provided it has been correctly completed, it will issue the petition and send a copy to you. The court will also send a copy of the petition to the Respondent, together with an acknowledgment of service form.

4. The Respondent has to complete and send the acknowledgement of service form back to the court in 7 working days.

5. If Respondent consents to the petition going ahead, the Petitioner can then apply for decree nisi. The decree nisi doesn't end the marriage.

6. Once decree nisi is pronounced, the Petitioner can apply for the decree nisi to be made absolute 6 weeks and 1 day from the date the decree nisi was pronounced. Once decree absolute has been granted, the marriage is dissolved.

7. The Respondent can apply for decree absolute three months from the date upon which the Petitioner could if the Petitioner fails to do so.

Divorce Dissolution and Separation Act 2020

The Government has reformed the law relating to divorce and a new No-fault Divorce will come into being in the Autumn of 2021.

The No-fault Divorce will offer some benefits to those wishing to get divorced. It will remove the "blame game", which means that no reasons will need to be given as to why the marriage broke down.

It will also stop the other spouse from contesting the divorce and should make the process more straightforward. The no -fault divorce should make the process simpler, faster and less costly for those wishing to get divorced.

There will be some changes with the terminology too. The process will be called an "application" for divorce rather than a "petition", so the person who starts the process will be called the "applicant" instead of the "petitioner". Instead of the "decree nisi" there will now be a "conditional order" and instead of the "decree absolute" there will be the "final order".

There will be a minimum period of 20 weeks between the initial application for divorce and the conditional order. And a further 6 weeks between the conditional and final order.

The minimum period is set to give couples the opportunity to really think carefully if they want to go ahead with the divorce and to give some thought about the practical issues involved if the divorce does go ahead.

The rules on financial and children issues remain the same.

Divorce online

In order to simplify the divorce process and make it less stressful for anyone who wants to get divorce, the Government has set up an online process. Currently you can apply for divorce online using the Government's website https://www.gov.uk/apply-for-divorce.
Once you've completed the online process, you can if you prefer download a copy of your petition (Form D8) and send the required copies of your petition, together with the court fee by post to the court.service. You can find out your local court service by checking on the Government's website, using the above link.

Although the divorce process itself is reasonably straightforward and you should be able to complete the petition yourself, it is always good to seek some legal advice or help from a family solicitor or a divorce coach before submitting the divorce petition to the court even though your spouse is in agreement with you.

THE 5 FACTS OF DIVORCE
& SOME CRAZY REASONS FOR DIVORCE

In order to apply for a divorce, you have to be married for a year. The ground for divorce is that the marriage must have irretrievably broken down due to one of the five facts which are as follows: -

1. Adultery & Intolerability
This fact can be relied upon if there has been sexual intercourse between your husband or wife with a person of the opposite sex. It is not enough if your husband and wife has just been speaking to

someone else on the telephone. In this case, as well as giving a short statement as to when and where the adultery took place, the petitioner also has to state that they find it intolerable to continue living with the respondent.

2. Unreasonable behaviour

This fact can be relied upon if your husband or wife has behaved badly in such a way that you cannot reasonably be expected to live with them.

To prove this fact, you have to give some examples where your husband or wife have behaved badly.

You can give details of arguments that have taken place, any incidents of bad behaviour, if there has been physical, verbal or emotional abuse then this can be stated. The behaviour must be

considered such that you cannot reasonably be expected to live with with your husband or wife. to rely on this fact.

3. Two years' separation

If you and your spouse have been separated for more than two years, then you can rely on this fact. However, at the end of the two year period, your spouse will need to consent to the divorce.

4. Desertion

If your spouse has deserted, you for more than two years and you do not know where your spouse is you may be able to rely on this fact. Intention to desert needs to be proved. This may be difficult so one of the other facts may have to be used instead.

5. Five years separation

If you and your spouse have separated for more than 5 years, then you can rely on this fact. You do not need your spouse's consent.

You will still need to go through the steps of a divorce as the divorce is not automatic which a lot of people think it would be.
Your spouse will still need to be served with the petition, although in some cases this may not be possible if you don't know where they are. There are ways that the court can deal with situations.-like this. It will just take a little longer to deal with.

Crazy reasons for divorce

There have been some crazy reasons that people have used when getting divorced. Here are some of them:

- A German woman divorced her husband for knocking down a wall and rebuilding a new wall as he stated the old one was dirty.

- A wife divorced her husband for eating peas with bread instead of a fork.

- A husband divorced his wife a few days after their wedding as he saw her without makeup and didn't recognise her.

- A wife divorced her Russian husband after he ran out of money whilst playing poker and he bet his wife.

- An Italian husband divorced his wife because he believed she was possessed by a devil.

- A wife divorced her husband for being too nice.

- A husband secretly divorced his wife during a trip, and she found out 22 years later. The husband claimed that he was trying to protect the wife's assets.

- A wife divorced her husband because he did not like the movie "Frozen".

- A husband divorced his wife when he discovered that his wife had plastic surgery and that she looked completely different before surgery. It was only after they had children, he had suspicions as the children looked completely different from his wife.

- A wife divorced her husband because he insisted that his mother goes with them on their honeymoon.

- A husband had an affair. His wife heard their parrot saying the word divorce and be patient. When the wife confronted the husband, he admitted to the affair.

Here are some interesting facts about divorce worldwide:

- Did you know that the oldest divorcee was 101 years old and from East Sussex in the UK? He divorced his 65-year-old wife in November 1980.

- In America there is one divorce that takes place approximately every 36 seconds. So, if you want to get divorced then live in America as the chances of you getting divorced are very high.

- India has the world's lowest divorce rate. India is the place to live in if you do not want a divorce.

- In Malta it takes 4 years for a divorce.

- In the US there are 100 divorces every hour.

- In the UK a survey was conducted and 50% of divorcees regretted their decision to divorce. Wow that is a lot.

- Nearly half of the divorce proceedings in Italy mention the app WhatsApp. We all know how addicted we are and use this app.

- If you have a lavish wedding, you are more likely to get divorced so best not to spend too much at your wedding.

- If you have children, you are less likely to get divorced. However, if you have twins or triplets then the chances of getting divorced increases so no twins or triplets.

- There was a study in Sweden that found that if you spend more than 45 minutes travelling you are more likely to get divorced.

- If you argue about finances, then you are more likely to get divorced.

- 6% of women admit to nearly leaving their spouse because of their mess and wish that their spouse was more organ-

- ized. Some men are therefore being forced to keep their belongings in the garden shed because women are taking up to two thirds of the space indoors. We all know women love shopping and need the space for their personal belongings.

CHAPTER 10

TIPS FOR DIVORCE

It's always useful to be prepared and here are some tips to think about.before you start divorce proceedings:.

1. It is best to obtain legal advice early as possible so that you become aware of your legal rights and your options. Do not make any decisions until you know your full rights and options.

2. Do not hide any details from your solicitor as your solicitor is there to help you achieve the best outcome. Your solicitor will not be able to help you to the best of their ability if they do not know the full facts of your case.

3. If you are about to purchase a property with your spouse, it is best to try to have your name placed on the deeds and mortgage too if possible.

4. If a property is in your spouse's sole name and the marriage breaks down, then you should register a matrimonial home's rights notice immediately to prevent your spouse from selling the property.

5. If a property is purchased it is always good to keep a copy of the conveyancing file. Best to have an electronic copy in a safe place so that you have easy access to it if required. Do bear in mind that solicitors only keep files for a specific period of time after which they are destroyed and therefore the file may not be available at a later date and even if it is you may have to pay a small fee to obtain the file from the solicitor.

6. Do not accept any offers that are made from your spouse until you have sight of the other's full and frank financial disclosure as you want to make sure you are getting the best settlement for yourself.

7. It is best to enter into a prenuptial agreement which can save a lot of costs, time and stress in the event that the

8. marriage breaks down. It is not too late if you are already married you can enter into a postnuptial agreement.

9. Do keep hold of your marriage certificate and other important documentation. Keep them in a safe place and somewhere easy for you to access. You will require your marriage certificate if you want to get divorced.

10. Do not share passwords with your spouse and regularly change them. If you are going to use your spouse's laptop, computer, iPad etc. then do log out once you have finished.

11. Do not sign any legal documents without seeking independent legal advice first. Make sure you fully understand what you are signing. Do not sign on a blank piece of paper no matter how much you trust your spouse.

12. Keep a note of your spouse's assets such as the addresses of the properties, bank account details, details of any valuable items etc.

13. If you can, keep up communication with your spouse on a neutral basis, especially when there are children involved. Family mediation is available and can help where there are disagreements about the division of finances and/or care of the children. A mediator is a third party and not on any one's side. The mediator will listen to the views of both you and your spouse and help you to reach an agreement for yourselves and for the benefit of the children.

14. Accept the reality of your situation and take steps to learn how to deal with your hurt, anger and loss and manage your emotions. A divorce coach or a stress specialist may help. Get the help you need and do not suffer alone.

15. Take your time when making decisions especially big decisions. Do your best to take the time you need to make proper decisions in your divorce even when your spouse is pressuring you to move faster. The more important the decision the more time you need to consider it carefully as it will affect the rest of your life. Book a session with a

16. divorce coach to talk things through if you are finding it difficult to deal with what you are being asked.

17. If you are holding a property in joint names with your spouse as joint tenants, then bear in mind that if something were to happen to you then your share will automatically go to your spouse. You may not want this to happen especially if you are going through a divorce.

You therefore should consider severing the tenancy so that it is held as tenants in common. However, it will be necessary for you to make a will to state who you want your share to go to in the event that something was to happen to you. You should talk to your solicitor about this.

CHAPTER 11

HOW TO DEAL WITH CHALLENGES

"Running away from any problem only increases the distance from the solution" Anon.

Whether you started the divorce process, or your partner did, there will be challenges along the way which can throw you off kilter. This is why it is so important to have a plan and to be able to know how to manage stress, so you can remain in control of your situation.

Every divorce is different because it is based on the particular marriage in question, not someone else's marriage. And whilst friends and family may have experienced divorce themselves and keep chipping in with advice from their experience, their experience will not necessarily be your experience.

There are however some challenges that are common to divorce such as:

- Divorce myths
- Arguing over trivial things
- Arrangements for the children
- Dealing with a difficult spouse

DIVORCE MYTHS

When I was working as a family lawyer, I came across many of what can only be described as "divorce myths".

You've probably heard of some of them, and maybe you can tell fact from fiction (or myth) or maybe not.

For example:
- You're soon to be ex tells you that they are entitled to 50% of everything in the marriage......Are they?
- You're soon to be ex tells you that they'll get everything because of your behaviour during the marriage....... will they?

- Your soon to be ex tells you that they don't want a divorce, and if they don't sign the paperwork it won't go ahead….is that right?

If you're thinking about divorce, or going through it, it's useful to know the facts. Because if you know the facts, you'll know how to separate facts from fiction when others try and tell you their version of what they think will happen.

Here are some further myths that Farzana has come across:
There are a number of myths with divorce, which I believe is important to clear up. The myths can deter someone from deciding to get divorced to wanting a quick divorce.

- **You can get divorced within seconds or days.**
We hear this in the media that famous couples get divorced in a matter of seconds or days. This is not true and there is no such thing as a quickie divorce. On average the divorce can take approximately 4 to 6 months providing there are no delays in the court's processing the divorce but most often than not I have seen divorces on average take 6 to 8 months to conclude.

- **If you get divorced, then you will get half of the other spouse's assets.**
It is not automatic that you will get half of your spouse's assets if you apply for a divorce. The starting off point in financial matter is 50-50% but the court takes a number of factors into account when deciding how the assets should be split for example how long the parties have been married for, what are the housing needs of the parties, what financial contributions have been made, what is in the earning capacity of the parties, health positions of the parties etc. The court can make an order for an unequal split.

- **If I do not sign the divorce, then the other spouse cannot get a divorce.**
It is still possible for a spouse to obtain a divorce even if one does not complete and sign the acknowledgement of service form. It just means that the person applying for a divorce will need to make additional applications and it will take longer to obtain the divorce. However, now that no fault divorce is coming into place in Autumn 2021 it will make it easier for a person to get divorced.

- **She is going to take me to the cleaners, and I will get nothing.**

Men often believe that their wives will get everything. Men do complain stating that what is the point of litigating when she is going to get everything. Although the wife may get a bigger share, men do also get a share of the assets. The upper hand is usually with the person who the children are living with or will live with once the divorce takes place.

- **If I cannot see the children, then I do need to pay child maintenance.**

Money issues and having contact with children are two separate issues. You should not stop paying child maintenance even if the other parent does not allow you to see the children. You can apply to the court for a child arrangements order for contact so that you can see the children.

- **A child gets to choose which parent they live with.**

The court can take the child's wishes and feelings into account. However, there is a number of factors that the court will consider before making a decision who the child should live with and the decision is not dependent on the child's wishes. The court will consider what is in the best interest of the child.

- **I do not have any assets here in the UK, so I am safe.**

This is not true. The courts can make an order in respect of assets that are abroad, and any assets abroad can be taken into account by the court in the matrimonial pot.

- **If your spouse commits adultery you get more money**

This is also not true. The courts rarely take the bad conduct of a spouse into account. Fault has no bearing on the financial matter unless conduct is taken into account by the court which has to be severe.

- **If you want a divorce, then you have to go to court**

If a husband and wife both consent to the divorce, then there is no need for them to attend court as a divorce can be obtained without going to court.

The property is in my name, so my spouse is not entitled to a share of it.

This is false. The court has the power to make an order for the property to be transferred to the other spouse or for it to be sold and for the proceeds of sale to be divided.

If I got married abroad then I cannot get divorced in the UK

In many cases it is possible to get divorced in the UK provided the court has jurisdiction to deal with the divorce. The marriage must be lawful in the country abroad where the marriage ceremony took place.

Arguing Over Trivial Things

Don't score points. It's not worth it. Why do some people argue over a teapot that isn't particularly valuable? It's usually because they don't have control over what's happening in their life right now so having control over a teapot gives them comfort. Or they may feel it gives them control over the other person. It costs time, energy and a lot of money to argue over trivia. Don't be drawn into it. Talk things through with your trusted friend or adviser and work out the best strategy for dealing with situations like this.

Dealing with a Difficult Spouse

You're stressed out by their argumentative behaviour. Their lack of empathy - when they started the process in the first place - or their determination to make things difficult for you, now you've seen the light and want to leave the marriage.

They're controlling and trying to get their way all the time. They may be being vengeful, and you may feel they are "out to get you" or perhaps they're being passive aggressive. In fact, you may recognise some of these traits in your behaviour if you're honest with yourself.

There are all types of emotions flying around during the divorce process for both of you.

Your spouse will be going through pretty much the same emotions as you, even though they may have instigated the divorce in the first place.

They may be at a different stage of the emotional process than you and want to move on more quickly, or they may be burying their head in the sand. The thing is, they aren't you, and you cannot possibly predict how they are feeling, any more than they can predict how you are feeling. The only person's behaviour you can predict is your own. You can only control what YOU do.

You might be thinking "if I do this, it'll make them do that". Don't bank on it. You are much better off using your energy wisely and productively rather than trying to second guess what they'll do.

So, what can you do go forward?

Here are some tips on how to react that will get you where you want to be without having to be fuelled with resentment and anger:

- Don't focus on what they do. Focus on how you can react in the best way to get the best outcome for you. If you need some help with this, talk it through with your trusted friend or divorce coach. It's important that you vent your anger and emotional feelings first so that you can make better decisions.

- Keep a diary and make notes of any problems that arise. Make sure you note the time and keep everything factual and to the point. Don't bring emotions into it. Be objective. What actually happened as opposed to what you believe should have happened. You may need to write it down twice - the first time to get all the emotional attachment out of your head. Then read it through and extract the bare facts of the situation.

- Do whatever it takes to keep calm. Learn how to handle your emotions effectively so that you can concentrate on the outcome you want. Talk things through with someone you trust. Find some relaxation techniques that work for you. Not all techniques work for everyone, but there will be some that you'll resonate with. For example, I find doing a Tai Chi or Yoga class a good way to relax my mind and calm my body. A massage can help relieve tension. A walk-in nature - in a park, by the sea. A warm bath with Epsom salts and essential oils such as lavender, rose, frankincense.

- Make sure you are getting enough rest. If you're finding it difficult to sleep, there are some great apps out there that you can listen to, to help you relax and drift off.

- If as time goes on, they continue to be difficult, pursue bad behaviour with objective energy. You can take action, refuse to be the victim and put yourself in the best position to succeed. Talking things through and working out your own plan of action will help you.

- Make sure you get some support. You don't have to do this on your own.

Those emotions keep creeping in

There will be times when you think that you're really getting to grips with things and then suddenly you find yourself in floods of tears. This is a normal reaction. Don't bottle it up or suppress it. That will not serve you. Go with the flow. Acknowledge the feelings and do something that makes you feel good, like a walk-in nature where you can let it all out.

The tears will stop eventually as your healing progresses. Richmond Park was my place to go. I'd sometimes find myself bent over with grief as the tears flowed. But as time went on, there were less tears and eventually I managed a whole walk in the park without crying.

Arrangements for Children

With all the emotions you are experiencing yourself, it can be hard to focus on helping your children with their emotions too. This is why it is so important that you find someone you can talk to.

If you've ever flown on a plane, you'll know that at some point before takeoff the steward will show you an oxygen mask and explain how to put it on. They'll also tell y

ou that you must put your mask on first before you help others. Likewise, you need to put your oxygen mask on first before you can help your children. So, make sure you have someone that you can talk through your concerns with, so that you'll get your emotions under control so that you'll be able to help children deal with the family break up with love and understanding.

Please don't treat your children as 'belongings' to be shared at certain times. They are their own individual unique selves, and you are both their parents.

As with adults, all children are different and will react differently to any situation depending upon their life experiences so far. Some will be upset, angry and feel it's their fault that their parents are splitting up. Others may show no reaction and others may even feel relieved.

These are all normal responses. They need to know that it's ok for them to feel whatever they are feeling and working things through with them with love and understanding will help them come to terms with what is going on around them.

Children don't have any control over what's happening and may feel vulnerable and upset. If they get angry and throw tantrums, help them understand their feelings and behaviours and look at different ways of expressing them.

It's important to refer to the behaviour itself rather than criticising the child. For example, it's ok to be angry and cross but it's not ok to punch your little brother. Help them find appropriate ways to express anger, such as talking to someone they trust, writing things down in a journal or hitting a cushion or pillow.

They may feel sad and unhappy and want you to get back together. This is understandable because they feel the familiarity of their world is falling apart. Acknowledge how they feel and be gentle in explaining why this isn't going to happen. Focus on good outcomes for the future.

Be honest with them in a way that they will understand according to their age. Don't blame the divorce on your spouse. It's important that they know that it's not their fault that you are splitting up.

Even if you disagree about everything else, encourage your spouse to work with you to support your children through the divorce.

Agreeing a parenting plan, with visits and rules in each home can really help everyone know what they are supposed to do and where they are supposed to be at any given time. Different parents have different rules because they are different people. One may be more flexible than the other. It can be very disconcerting for a child to have to go to bed at 8 pm in one household and 7.30 pm in another. Is there a compromise you can make to be more consistent between you so that your children are not confused?

Make sure that you both have clothes, books and toys at both properties, so the children have familiar things around them. Have a special bag that they can pack to include all the things they need to take between homes, such as their special toy, their phone, schoolwork etc.

If you are genuinely concerned about the welfare of your children if they stay with the other person, you should flag up your concerns. For example, my ex was an alcoholic and frequently used to drive whilst under the influence of alcohol. I was really worried that he would drink and drive whilst having contact, so the court added a clause in the contact order that he should not drink alcohol when he had contact with the children.

However, if your ex likes taking the children to football and feeding them a McDonalds once every now and then and you don't, that's not a reason for you to cause problems with their contact.

EXERCISE 8 - What challenges might come up for me?

Divorce Challenge		
Challenge	What can I do to work through it?	What support might I need?

Use this chart to plan your challenges, how you can work through them and what support you might need.

CHAPTER 12

SECTION 25 FACTORS & ORDERS

Section 25 Matrimonial Causes Act 1973

There are many people that are reluctant in issuing divorce proceedings as they are worried about what would happen to their home, children and how they would cope with the finances. These things do stop people from applying for divorce and many people continue to live unhappy lives.

Financial proceedings can be daunting and complex. However, if you have the right solicitor instructed then they can assist you to overcome any fears or anxiety that you may have.

So how do courts decide what each spouse gets from the financial settlement. Well, there are a number of factors that the court takes into account. The factors can be found under Section 25 of the Matrimonial Causes Act 1973. The court looks at the following: -

a) The income, earning capacity, property and other financial resources which each of the parties to the marriage has or is likely to have in the foreseeable future, including in the case of earning capacity any increase in that capacity which it would in the opinion of the court be reasonable to expect a party to the marriage to take steps to acquire. How much longer you can continue to work until you reach retirement age will be looked at.

b) The financial needs, obligations and responsibilities which each of the parties to the marriage has or is likely to have in the foreseeable future. What your current expenses are and what your future expenses are will be looked at.

c) The standard of living enjoyed by the family before the breakdown of the marriage. How your lifestyle was prior to the breakdown will be taken into account and you could argue that you need to continue to live the same lifestyle.

d) The age of each party to the marriage and the duration of the marriage.

e) The contributions which each of the parties has made or is likely in the foreseeable future to make to the welfare of the family, including any contribution by looking after the home or caring for the family. If you have contributed for example towards the purchase of the family home, paid for any repairs or renovations done, being paying for bills etc. then this can be taken into account.

f) The conduct of each of the parties if that conduct is such that it would in the opinion of the court be inequitable to disregard it. The bad conduct of a party is rarely taken into account unless the conduct is really bad.

g) In the case of proceedings for divorce or nullity of marriage, the value of each of the parties to the marriage of any benefit which by reason of the dissolution or annulment of the marriage, that party will lose the chance of acquiring.

The court will look at the above before making a decision as to how the assets are to be divided.

Many cases are usually a "needs based" case. This means the court looks at what the parties will need to live on going forward. Therefore, even if you have made a lot of financial contributions the court is going to be more concerned with how the needs of the parties will be met. Usually, the person whom the children will live with may receive more as they will need to house themselves and the children.

What orders can the Court make?

In financial proceedings the court has power to make a wide range of orders. The court will consider the Section 25 factors and will then make a decision as to what orders should be made.

- Where there are young children and if there is not much equity in the family home to sell the same and for both parties to be re-housed or buy the other one out, the court tends to make a "Mesher" Order. A Mesher Order is where the court allows the spouse who is looking after the children to stay in the family

- home until the youngest child reaches 18 or finishes full time education. The court can have trigger events put in place where the family home is sold earlier for example if the spouse in the property remarries, or one of them dies etc.

- The court can order for a property to be sold and for the proceeds of sale to be divided between the parties and not necessarily in equal shares. The parties can then use the proceeds from their share if they wish to purchase housing for themselves.

- The court can make an order for a lump sum payment to be made by one spouse to another spouse.

- The court could order for periodical payments often referred to as spousal maintenance to be paid to one spouse by another.

- The court also has power to make an order for a pension sharing order.

- The court will consider whether a case is suitable for a clean break. If a clean break order is made it means that the parties would have no financial claim against the other.

- The court will ensure that the children will be housed appropriately especially if they are really young.

CHAPTER 13

STEPS IN FINANCIAL PROCEEDINGS & CHECKLIST

This section covers cases about Financial Remedy for couples who are divorcing. This is a simple guide to the procedure. The full procedure is contained in Part 9 of the Family Procedure Rules, which can be found here: https://www.justice.gov.uk/courts/procedure-rules/family/rules_pd_menu.

Mediation

Before an application for financial proceedings is made to the Court, you will need to attend a mediation meeting (unless you are exempt from doing so). This meeting is referred to as an "MIAM" (Mediation Information Assessment Meeting).

The mediation service you approach will check that your case is suitable for mediation. If it is, you will usually attend a MIAM on your own with the mediator.

The mediator will work with you to identify any problems you may have with the division of the finances and will help you work towards an agreement. You may have already reached an agreement with your spouse and just want to talk things through with a professional before committing to the financial agreement.

You can check online for family mediation centres at https://www.familymediationcouncil.org.uk/find-local-mediator/. Enter your postcode and you'll find a list of mediators near to you. They will need to be registered MIAM mediators.

Mediation centres do charge fees for mediation and some will check if you qualify for legal aid. If your spouse is willing to mediate, then you should engage in the process of mediation as this will be more cost effective and quicker.

If an agreement is reached at mediation, then a consent order can then be drafted in terms of the mediation agreement which will need to be signed by both of you and then filed at court to be approved so that it becomes legally binding. This consent order can include a 'clean break' which means that neither of you can claim against the other in respect of this marriage once the order is made. The courts are asking for the consent orders to be lodge using the HMCTS online portal. Many solicitors have started using the portal, but it is in its early stages.

Financial Proceedings

If you have attended mediation and were unable to come to an agreement, you will then have to apply for the finances of the marriage to be determined by the court.

First of all, you will need to complete Form A and send it to the court with Form FM1 (signed by a mediator or signed by a solicitor/litigant in person giving reasons why mediation was not possible) together with the court fee of £255.00. This court fee is current during the publishing of this book. Court fees change so you need to check the up-to-date fees at https://www.gov.uk/court-fees-what-they-are.

It does not matter who starts the divorce proceedings, either of you can apply for a financial order. The person making the application will be known as the Applicant and the person receiving the application will be known as the Respondent.

Once it has received your application and fee and checked everything is in order, the Court will issue the application and set down the date for a First Directions Appointment (FDA).

This is the first hearing in connection with resolving the outstanding financial issues. During this hearing, the court will be focusing on identifying the issues in dispute and what steps that need to be taken before a final decision can be reached.

The court doesn't always resolve things at a first hearing, although it may be possible. Strict timescales will now apply, which will be set out in the Notice of First Appointment which will be sent to both you and your spouse. This notice will include some key dates and actions that you both have to follow with regard to completing and filing the following documents.

Disclosure

Before the hearing, you'll both have to disclose certain information to each other and the court. You'll need to complete a financial statement in Form E and send it to one another and the court. Form E is a comprehensive statement of your jobs(s), earnings, savings, pensions, property, expenditure and debts.

You'll have to obtain various documents, such as up to date valuations and bank statements (see checklist below) to complete the form and copies of these documents will need to be attached to it.

Once Form E has been sent and received, you may have some questions that you want to clarify as to what is included or hasn't been included in your spouse's Form E. (There may be some bank accounts that you believe they haven't disclosed or some debts that you haven't heard of previously). These questions will need to be raised bearer the first hearing by way of a Questionnaire raising specific questions for your spouse to answer.

Also before the FDA takes place, you will both have to draw up a chronology of your marriage, giving details of the key dates and events, Statement of Costs, together with a Statement of Issues This statement usually sets out the main issues of the case what you agree with, what you are still in disagreement about so that the Judge can see what you haven't been able to work out and concentrate on helping you both find a resolution.

First Directions Appointment Hearing (FDA)

If disclosure is complete and everything seems to be relatively straightforward, this FDA can also be used as a Financial Dispute Resolution (FDR) hearing to save time and costs and where agreement may be reached and incorporated into a consent order.

However, if there are still disputes over certain issues that cannot be resolved without further information, the judge will make directions for you and your spouse to comply with so that next time the FDR can proceed. This can include getting further information such as pension valuations, medical reports, valuations of property for example).

Financial Dispute Resolution Hearing (FDR)

The FDR is an opportunity for you and your spouse to work out an agreement in relation to the finances of your marriage. The majority of cases are usually resolved by agreement at or before an FDR.

The Judge becomes much more involved in an FDR hearing and will express provision views on how he/she sees disagreements between you and your spouse being decided at a later hearing. The Judge does not make a decision at the FDR. It is for you and your spouse to make your decisions. The Judge is there to guide you and suggest what may happen in any further hearings and will make particular reference to ongoing costs.

If you are still in disagreement at the end of the FDR, the Judge dealing with it will not be able to take further part in your case. This is to allow the judge to be able to speak freely during the hearing and it could prejudice any further hearings if the Judge were to continue with your case.

Final Hearing

If you still cannot agree, a date will be set for a final hearing, which is in effect a trial. The Judge listens to the evidence provided by you and your spouse and then makes a decision. As this is a full hearing, bundles of documents will have to be prepared by both you and your spouse, exchanged with each other and filed with the Court.

In this hearing, it's the Judge who reaches the final decisions and what he or she decides may be different from what you and your husband initially wanted for yourselves. The Judge has power to make orders to delay a property sale, sell or transfer property, share pensions, pay lump sums or monthly maintenance.

This process can take a long time and if you can reach an agreement without involving the court it will save you time, money and be emotionally less painful.

COVID-19

Due to lockdown, many hearings have been and are continuing to take place remotely. However, not all hearings are suitable to be dealt with remotely and therefore some hearings are taking place face to face where parties are being asked to attend Court with their representatives.

If a remote hearing is taking place, then the Court usually confirms the method for this a few days before the hearing. Remote hearing can take place via telephone, Skype, Microsoft Teams, video (CVP) etc. See Chapter 16 for more information on attending court in person and virtually.

Checklist of Documents Required for Form E

Financial Statement in Form E may seem a bit of a challenge to complete; however, it is a very useful document because it sets out all the finances of the marriage in one place.   If you get your supporting documents together before you start completing it, you'll find it much easier to work through.

Here's a list of the documents you'll need to complete your Form E:

- Copy valuation of all properties owned solely or jointly, dated within the last 6 months.

- Recent mortgage statement confirming the sum outstanding on each mortgage.

- Copies of bank statement for the last 12 months of each bank account held solely or jointly in the UK and abroad.

- Documentary evidence of any investments such as giving details of values of shares, bonds, stocks, unit trusts, investment trusts etc.

- Copy of any endowment policies or life policies.

- Documentary evidence of any monies owed to you.

- Documentary evidence of any items worth more than £500.00, showing the value of the items.

- Documentary evidence of all liabilities, such as credit and store card debts, loans, hire purchase agreements, etc.

- Copies of all business accounts for the last 2 financial years.

- Documentary evidence of the cash equivalent transfer value of any pensions.

- P60 and last three pay slips.

- Last P11D if one has been issued.

- Copy of the last tax assessment or letter from accountant confirming tax liability.

- A copy of the management accounts if net income from the last financial year and estimated net income for the next 12 months is different.

- Evidence of any dividends, interest or rental income received.

- Evidence of any state benefits received.

CHAPTER 14

CHILDREN AND DIVORCE

Divorce is one of the hardest things for any family to overcome especially for children. Not only are the husband and wife affected but the children are too, says Farzana.

I have seen many parents fight over their children in divorce battles. Why would not they as children are important. However, children should not be treated as tools to get back at the other spouse. Unfortunately, this happens and at the end of the day it is the children who suffer.

I have represented many fathers as well as mothers in children proceedings. A lot of fathers have been desperate to see their children. Some of them have gone from spending normal days with their children, being involved in their upbringing to suddenly not being able to see their children due to an incident occurring.

Unfortunately, some fathers have had false allegations made against them where they have been arrested or kicked out of their own home by their spouse. They have had to rely on the court system in order to get to see their children. The allegations that I have come across are of domestic violence, sexual abuse, emotional abuse, being a terrorist and teaching child to become a terrorist etc. Others have had to have lengthy and expensive court proceedings before they have been able to see their children.

There have also been cases where one parent has coached their children to say they don't want to see the other parent. Some children are too scared to upset the parent that they are living with to say they want to see the other parent.

Some mothers have suffered abuse from the fathers. They are desperate to safeguard their children from the fathers. I represented a mother who separated from her spouse after their child alleged the father had sexually abused her. Social services were involved who took the child away and I fought to get the child back to the mother which did happen. The father applied to have contact with the child through the court.

You can imagine how devastated and frightened the mother would have been who just wanted to protect her child.

I believe that the court system does need to be changed. The proceedings can be lengthy especially if allegations are raised and children miss out in seeing one parent which is not good for their mental wellbeing. I believe a child should have contact with both parents unless there are very good reasons not to do so. A child can be affected in many ways especially when they grow older. I have seen children as young as 5 having counselling when that is an age for them to enjoy, play and be carefree.

So, what can parents do? Well, they can attend a separated parents information program to help them see how conflict with the other parent can impact their child

The programme is usually referred to as "SPIP". It is a short course which usually lasts for a couple of hours. You do not need to attend the course with the other parent. You are usually booked to attend at separate dates and times.

The court can make an order for both parents to attend the programme. If the court does this then the activity provider will make direct contact with each parent to book the programme. If the court makes an order to attend the programme then it is usually free to attend.

However, if you book the programme without the court making an order then there may be a fee to pay. The activity provider will usually provide you with a certificate once the programme is completed, which you can use as evidence to show that you have attended the same.

Parents can try talking to each other and try to reach an agreement without having to drag the matter through the courts. Mediation is available to parents. Mediators are independent third parties that listen to the views of the parents in order to help them reach an agreement.

There are many parenting courses available that can be undertaken, and a parenting plan can be put in place so that everyone knows who is doing what, when and where.

CHAPTER 15

STEPS IN CHILD ARRANGEMENTS ORDER PROCEEDINGS

AND ORDERS

This chapter provides a guide to the Child Arrangements Programme. For the full programme go to Practice Direction 12B Child Arrangement Programme here: https://www.justice.gov.uk courts/procedure-rules/family/practice_directions/pd_part_12b

Parents and/or carers of children are usually able to start proceedings without obtaining permission from the court. However, if there is an additional early stage where you have to seek permission of the court to bring an application (seeking 'leave' of the Court), you will need to make your application on Form C2.

Mediation

Before making an application to the Court, all applicants must initially attend MIAM (Mediation Information Assessment Meeting unless exempt from doing so. The aim of the MIAM meeting is to see if the problem you want to ask the Court to resolve can be settled by mediation. If your case isn't suitable for mediation or it cannot be resolved during mediation, the mediator will confirm this and allow you to carry on and make your application to the Court.

Application Process

You will then need to make an application to the Court using Form C100. You need to complete this form with details of the orders you wish to apply for and brief reasons for the application. This will set the court timetable in motion. If you are making the application, you will be known as the Applicant. The other party will be known as the Respondent.

You may also need to complete Form C1A if you believe that there are issues surrounding safeguarding, welfare, harm, danger etc to the children. It is really important that before you make any type of application you seek legal advice even if you want to try to deal with the matter yourself. There is nothing worse than completing a wrong application form or not applying for the relevant orders. It could cost more or cause delays to fix errors later on.

The application forms then need to be submitted to the Court with a Court fee (which is currently £215.00. You can check the current court fees at www.gov.uk.)

The Court will issue the application and list it for a First Hearing Dispute Resolution Appointment (FHDRA).

At least 14 days before this First Hearing, you will need to send all the documents to the other party. The other party should acknow-ledge receipt of the documents and complete their Answer form within 14 days of service. They can do this on Form C7.

CAFCASS (Children & Families Court Advisory Service)

Once the application has been issued CAFCASS (Children & Families Court Advisory and Support Service) will start making some basic safeguarding enquiries with the Police and Social Services. CAFCASS officers are officers of the court who are specialist social workers. They provide advice and recommenda-tions to the family courts in order to assist the judges to make a decision. Cafcass have the children's best interest to heart. They may get in touch with you to talk to you about any safety issues in relation to you or the children.

FHDRA (First Hearing Dispute Resolution Appointment)

The FHDRA will usually not be less than 4 weeks after the issue of the application in order to allow time for safeguarding checks. At the FHDRA, the Court will consider the safeguarding information and will encourage you and the other party to resolve your dispute by agreement. If the safeguarding information isn't available with-in the timescale, the Court may have to postpone the FHDRA until it is. If everything can be agreed at the FHDRA, the Court may make a final order and the case will end.

The Court will listen to both of you but won't hear any evidence. If you cannot completely resolve your dispute, it will give you Direc-tions to progress the case or get the case ready for a fuller hear ing. The Court won't always make temporary orders at this point. You can ask the Court to grant interim orders such as an interim order for contact. However, if there are serious allegations made against you, then the Court may be reluctant to grant the contact.

The Court can ask you both to go to MIAM if you haven't already done so. It may also order CAFCASS to prepare a report. This report can take up to 12 weeks to prepare and you may have to go back to Court a couple of weeks after the report is finished if

they are disputes about the fact that are important to the decision the Court has to make about the children. This can take the form of domestic abuse allegations that are denied for example.

Fact Finding Hearing

The Court may have to deal with these first and direct both of you to prepare written statements about the allegations in advance of a Fact-Finding Hearing. After a Fact-Finding Hearing, the Court can consider if it needs a report from CAFCASS based upon what the judge has decided did or did not happen.

During a Fact-Finding Hearing, both of you will give evidence, so this hearing may take longer than the FHDRA - perhaps half a day or a day.

Once the Court has received any recommendations from CAFCASS and has decided on what has happened in the past, you will be called to a Dispute Resolution Appointment to see if you can now agree your dispute. If you can, the process will end, and a final order will be made. If not, your case will be listed for a final hearing so you can give evidence. You may be asked to produce a formal statement.

Prior to the Final Hearing, you will have to prepare a bundle of all he papers and statements in the case. This is called the 'Court Bundle' and needs to be set out in a certain way. At this stage, the Court will also usually require an up-to-date summary, a position statement of what you want the Court to decide and a simple chronology. You can find out more about a Fact Finding Hearing in Chapter 17.

Final Hearing

The Final Hearing takes the form of a trial where both of you will give evidence and will be able to challenge each other's evidence by asking questions. The judge will listen to you both and then come to a decision. The judge decide what Orders should or should not be made as he/she considers appropriate.

This should be the end of the process. However, in some cases either of you may have to return to the Court to ask for an Order to be enforced if the other person is breaking it. Or if the Order needs to be changed because circumstances have changed, and you cannot agree.

What Orders can be applied for in children proceedings?

A Child Arrangements Order for Contact
This should be applied for if you want to see and have contact with your child.

A Child Arrangements Order for Residence (also known as live with order)
This should be applied for if you want your child to live with you.

A Child Arrangements Order for shared care
This can be applied for if you want the child to partly live with you and partly live with the other parent.

A Prohibited Steps Order
If you fear that the other parent is going to remove your child out of the jurisdiction of England and Wales and not bring the child back, then you can apply for this order.

A Specific Issues Order
This can be applied for if you want the other parent to do something such as provide you with the passport of the child or give your health information of a child etc. You should also apply for this order if you want the court to give you permission to relocate the child.

CHAPTER 16

ATTENDANCE AT COURT
IN PERSON AND VIRTUALLY

Having to attend court may sound scary and frightening but it does not have to be. Remember that judges, barristers and solicitors are all human beings at the end of the day. So, what's the difference between a solicitor and a barrister. Well, a solicitor usually has contact with a client throughout the case and usually prepares the case. A barrister (also known as counsel) usually represents a client at court hearings. Some solicitors also attend court and represent clients instead of a barrister. Judges make decisions.

Attendance in Person

If you have instructed a solicitor to represent you on your matter, then the solicitor will prepare for the court hearing. The solicitor will explain what type of hearing will take place, what to expect, whether or not you are required to give evidence. If you are not required to give evidence and a barrister or solicitor represents you at court, then you are not likely to have to speak. Your representative will speak on your behalf.

You can if you want take a friend or family member to court for moral support but they will not be allowed to attend the actual hearing. The hearings take place in private. Due to the Covid 19 pandemic a lot of hearings are taking place remotely via telephone, Skype, Microsoft Teams etc. The court will confirm which method will be used. If the hearing is to take place remotely then the court will usually send you a link or dial you in for the hearing. You just have to ensure that you make yourself available on the day of the hearing.

You will be expected to stand up when the judge arrives in the courtroom. The judge will have a court bundle containing the relevant documents for the hearing which usually the applicant's solicitors will send to the court a few days before the hearing. The udge would have read some of the documents prior to the hearing aking place.

There are different types of hearing depending on the type of matter and application made. It is usually at fact finding hearings or inal hearings that you are required to give evidence. This means you will be asked to go into the witness box and will be questioned.

Virtual Attendance at Court

As a result of the COVID-19 pandemic, Family Courts in England and Wales have resorted to online hearings to ensure that cases can continue in lockdown. Cases can now take part by telephone, Skype and video (Zoom) and are likely to continue to be the norm or some while yet. These hearings are referred to as "Remote Hearings".

If you have a solicitor acting for you, they should explain the process to you and make sure you have the necessary technology/ software.

Some useful tips for you to think about -

• You should be told by the Court which software will be used for the hearing (ie Zoom, Microsoft Teams, Skype), Make sure that you have access to it. You may have to download the software onto your computer/laptop.

• If it's possible, plug your lap top/computer/phone into the mains rather than just rely on the battery. That way you don't have to worry about whether the battery will run out during the hearing. It can also help with a more stable internet connection.

• Use headphones with a microphone if you can. This helps with privacy and also reduces background noise.

• Check the environment where you are going to join the hearing. Ideally you should be in a private room away from anyone who may interrupt you during the hearing. If you have children, it's a good idea to arrange child care for them.

- What's your internet speed like in the area you have chosen? Can you get a good signal?

- Make sure that you can communicate effectively with your legal team during the hearing. This may be by email, WhatsApp or a video chat. It's useful to have two devices - one to deal with the court hearing and the other to communicate with your legal team. For example, you could use your computer for the hearing and your phone for your legal team.

- Make a list of what you need during the hearing as you won't be able to leave once it starts. What paperwork will you need to refer to? Have you got copies of everything you need?

- Remote hearings can be particularly intense and tiring due to the reliance on technology. Make sure you have a comfortable seat. A drink of water, note pad and pen and anything else you feel you may need during the course of the hearing.

- Once the hearing starts, you need to check that your device is muted to avoid any background noise being picked up in the courtroom.

- Just because you are at home, doesn't mean that you won't be seen. The Judge will be able to see you. So dress appropriately. It's important that you make a good impression. Do not smoke or drink alcohol whilst you are attending the hearing.

- Get settled in front of your device 10 minutes before you are due to log on to the hearing. Check that you have everything you need. Check the login details and check that you are connected to your legal team. Sit quietly with your feet on the floor and take some nice, deep breaths. If at any time you feel anxious during the hearing, take some deep breaths. Breathe gently in through your nose, fill up your lungs slowly and then exhale.

CHAPTER 17

WHAT IS A FACT-FINDING HEARING?

When is a Fact Finding Hearing Required?

Usually when one party makes allegations against the other party the court can list the case for a fact-finding hearing to determine if the allegations are true or not.

The court will ask the party that is making the allegations to prepare a document which is often referred to as the Scott's schedule. This document will need to list out the allegations against the other party and give a time frame as to when they happened. The other party will then be given an opportunity to respond to the allegations where they would respond to each allegation made. The court will also ask the parties to draft and provide witness statements to support their case.

It is common in children cases for a fact-finding hearing to be listed although it can be listed in other areas of family law such as in injunction proceedings. If the court believes it is necessary to hear the allegations and that they will make a difference to the court's decision, then this type of hearing will be listed.

You will need to attend the fact-finding hearing if one has been listed. The hearings can take place in person or remotely. The hearings can last from a day to a number of weeks depending on the number of allegations, number of witnesses to give evidence, how complex the case is, number of documents etc.

If the hearing is to take place in person then one by one each witness including the parties will be asked to go into the witness box where evidence will be heard. You will initially be asked to confirm your full name and address. You will also be referred to your statements and the court will want confirmation that you signed the statement and that it is correct. If you want to make any amendments to the statement, then you can inform the court at the time.

You will be asked questions by your own counsel and then the other party's counsel. The judge may interrupt at times and ask questions. Your own counsel will ask you further questions once the other party's counsel has finished asking you questions.

The judge will listen to the evidence of all parties including any witnesses. The judge will also consider the documents that have been filed with the court which will be contained in a court bundle for the hearing.

The judge will then make a decision by going through each allegation and confirming if the allegation is found against the person who has been alleged of the same. The judge will usually provide reasons of coming to the decision.

Being Prepared is Key

Being prepared for any hearing is so important. There is usually a lot of work that needs to be undertaken before any hearing takes place especially a fact finding or a final hearing. It is therefore important that you work with your solicitor to ensure that everything gets prepared in advance and this will no doubt give time for any person representing you at the hearing to prepare fully for the case.

Usually, a Court Bundle needs to be prepared for each hearing which the solicitor will prepare. It will depend on whether you are the applicant in the case or not and whether you have representation. Depending on the type of matter there are certain documents that need to be placed in the Court Bundle according to the practice directions.

CHAPTER 18

HOW TO SEEK PROTECTION IF YOU ARE A VICTIM OF DOMESTIC VIOLENCE

Suffering in silence is not the right thing to do if you are a victim of domestic violence. Although it may seem hard to get out of a situation and not knowing where you will go or how you will cope is difficult.

However, there are ways that you can seek protection to safeguard yourself and your children should you need to. If you are suffering from domestic violence whether its physical or even emotional or controlling behaviour then the first step you should take is to report the matter to the police.

You should ask the police to assist you. The police will usually provide you with a crime reference number once you report the matter. If they cannot assist you then the next step to do is seek advice from a family solicitor. You can call Refuge 24 hour helpline to help you understand your rights and options and how to find a family solicitor who can help you. (See "useful links" at the end of this book for details of Refuge).

The solicitor can help you to apply for a Non-Molestation Order. This is an order that can prevent the person who is harming you to stop from using violence, intimidating you, threatening you, encouraging anyone else to do the same on their behalf etc. You can even ask for provisions to be placed in the order so that the person does not make any contact with you such as send you a message via text, email or call you etc.

To apply for the order, you have to complete an application form and also draft a statement. The statement needs to give details of the problems that you have faced, give details of why you want to apply for the order, explain why there is a serious likelihood that a further incident will take place etc. If you are in real danger and have sufficient reasons you can apply for this order on an emergency basis without giving notice to the person harming, you.

You can also apply for an Occupation Order if you want a person to leave the property for example the spouse. The court will decide if they need to leave or not.

CHAPTER 19

THE FUTURE'S BRIGHT

You may be feeling that the future is anything but bright just now and that it holds a lot of unknowns says Margaret. You don't know where you'll live, how much money you'll have, what will people think of you, whether your friends will still be friends, how your family will react and how your children will cope.

It's natural to feel such fears in a situation such as divorce. And it's perfectly ok to feel that way. However, it serves no useful purpose to stay in that fear zone. Winston Churchill famously once said "If you're going through hell - keep going" and that's exactly what you need to do too.

If you keep going, moving forward, even with baby steps, you will get through this. Destination Divorce. It's like taking a long journey, walking the Camino for example. (Just in case you don't know, walking the Camino is a pilgrimage of some 500 miles or so, depending where you start, usually in France. The end of the journey is at Santiago de Compostela in Spain. If you're interested, there is a really good film about walking the Camino. It's called 'The Way', starring Martin Sheen).

Some days get tough where you have to walk up hills and mountains. It may be burning hot or pouring with rain and windy. So, you rest up for a couple of days to get your energy back - and then you start off again.

You may find that during your journey through divorce, you need to stop and rest for a while to get your energy back. And then start again. And remember, just like walking the Camino, you'll be starting again at a new starting point from where you first started your journey. You'll have hours of walking under your belt where you've learned new things, seen new scenery, got through challenging situations, understood things about yourself that you didn't know or you had forgotten and maybe developed new skills along the way.

Many of my coaching clients over the years had come through the divorce process, but simply didn't know what to do next. They were like rabbits in the headlights, they had been so overwhelmed and stressed about what was going on, that they failed to consider how they could make a future for themselves. I was in that situation too.

After the tremendous relief of my husband finally leaving the country, I had no idea what to do next. I had no plan. I had no vision of what my future could be. I had no friends and I felt stuck in a place where there was no exit. And you'll remember that I fell very ill for a long time.

Looking back, I wish I had thought more about what I could achieve in the future, rather than what I couldn't. I strongly believe that I would have felt in a much better position both physically and mentally. This is why I believe it's important for you, too, to take a look at what you can achieve, now the plans you thought you had for the future have changed dramatically due to your divorce.

One of my client's said to me in one of our sessions: "Everything is blank. There is not future to look at anymore. All my hopes and dreams of what we would do together are over: There is nothing to look forward to. I don't know what to do".

At first, we can't see anything because we are still dealing with the shock and stress of our situation. It's as if a thick fog has descended in front of us. We don't know now what's behind it - is it safe to walk through it or is there a precipice out there waiting for us to fall off? So, we stay this side of the fog where we believe it is safe. But what if we do push through the fog? Have you ever driven through fog? I absolutely hate it! I find I have to go really slowly and be completely focused on driving. Sometimes I have to stop and wait for a bit until it lifts a little and I can see more clearly. Or sometimes I'll come across another motorist in front of me, and I'll follow their taillights. It's a huge struggle, but in the end, I come through.

Once we get through the fog, the road is clear again and we don't have to focus quite so strongly. It's an immense relief.

Going back to my client, (to keep confidentiality, I'll call her Fay, which is not her real name) we talked about everything being blank and eventually we ended up with a blank sheet of paper in front of us. This was an opportunity to write a brand-new future. A future that could be as Fay wanted it to be, not according to how others felt she should live her life.

How many times have we done things because we felt we ought to? How many times have we not done things because we felt we ought not to? Usually, it's because we are trying to please someone else or our particular upbringing and perhaps our culture creates the notion that we must do things in a certain way. We criticise ourselves internally that "I should do this because…." "I shouldn't do that because…." What if you could write down all the things you'd like to do without those external and internal criticisms? What would that look like?

Fay started to work on this blank sheet of paper. It was difficult at first for her to think about where to start; however, with the help of some exercises I gave her, that blank sheet of paper started to fill up quickly with lots of thoughts, hopes and dreams about what her future could be.

Imagination is given to us so we can step outside of our personal limits and find our greatest potential. By not limiting her thinking to what she thought she should do, but what she'd love to do, expanded possibilities that she hadn't thought of before and drew opportunities towards her that she had previously missed.

So many people think that they are not good enough or not cut out to do certain things. Even though they would like to do them. I've heard people wistfully say after watching Masterchef, "I'd love to make that recipe, but I just couldn't do it, I'm not cut out to be a cook". And I say to them, but just for a moment think - what if you could? What if you could make that recipe? What would need to change? What would you need to be doing differently? What skills might you need? If you'd really like to make that meal, what is really stopping you? And the answer inevitably comes back to "me".

One of my clients (I'll call her Freda, not her real name) was afraid of going out and socialising after she was divorced. Before her husband left her for a younger model (as she put it) they'd had a busy social life. They belonged to the golf club and used to eat out there regularly and play golf. They'd go out every Friday night for a meal to celebrate the end of the week. Weekends were usually packed with activities from golf to socialising with friends.

After the divorce, many of these friends tailed off. They were the ones that were married and whom my client and her husband had visited as a couple. They didn't ask her round for supper anymore and any invitations she sent out were politely refused.

My client was at a very low ebb when she booked her first session with me. Her self-esteem had taken a huge knock. She had lost confidence in herself and hadn't been in a cafe or bar for a couple of years. Her social life was nil. She had got herself into a position where she was afraid to go out. She felt conspicuous if she went into a cafe on her own and ordered coffee. She felt everyone was staring at her. She would become so uncomfortable that she would walk out. Her home became her familiarity zone, which she found difficult to step out of. She had really had enough of feeling like this and wanted to go out, but just didn't know how to do it anymore.

Clearly, she had been able to leave her home as she had come to see me. (This was in the days when we had face to face meetings!). We talked for a while about what cafes and restaurants were in her area and she mentioned a couple of times a little Italian cafe where the proprietors were Italian and really welcoming - but of course she couldn't go in there because they would not want to welcome her anymore. I asked her whether she knew this to be true, and she replied that she hadn't actually been in the cafe since her divorce.

I asked her what she thought might happen if she did go into the cafe and ordered coffee? She said she thought that the proprietors might be cold towards her and ignore her, as they were very friendly with her husband. They had also been friendly towards her too in the past. So, I asked her what if they were friendly towards her as they had been previously? What if they welcomed her with open arms? How would that be? She said that would be a wonderful feeling - but of course they wouldn't do that would they?

We explored this further and looked at what the consequences could be if she took the step to go into the cafe. The proprietors may be welcoming, they may be cool towards her or they may refuse to serve her she thought. But if it did work, it was a really safe place to go where she'd felt really comfortable in the past on her own whilst waiting for her husband to join her.

We worked through the various scenarios of 'what happens if...' and what to do, particularly if they were cold towards her. I gave her some breathing and grounding exercises to do as well.
At our following session, my client was looking much brighter and happier.

She told me that she had taken a deep breath and gone into the cafe. The proprietors were over the moon to see her and made a complete fuss of her. They even gave her a free coffee! She started to chat to some of the other customers who were regulars and will be going back there again.

This small step, outside of the familiarity zone of her home, was enough to change that to a new familiarity zone of being able to go into the cafe. Just gently nudging into the new zone, creates a new zone to work from - just like starting at a different point in the Camino. She now has the experience of walking into the cafe and being prepared to face the consequences.

Eventually she headed out to restaurants by herself. She had found a new confidence. She would take a book with her or work on her device and felt completely at ease, whether with friends or on her own.

(Incidentally, if you'd like to know what she would have done if they had been cool towards her, it was this: "I shall walk in there, order coffee, and if they are off hand or offensive, I'll simply tell them I'm sorry I don't want the coffee after all and leave with my head held high". Because she faced her fear and had planned what to do in the event this may happen, she was able to take action).

Planning for the future

As with any type of planning, it's useful to have a starting point. Because once you have that no matter how bad it may seem to you at the moment, you have something to work from. It can also help you chart your progress - what's working well and what you might need to improve.

A good place to start is with the Wheel of Life. This is a really useful tool and I use it a lot in my coaching sessions. In the first session, it helps my clients understand how they feel at that point about certain parts of their life.

As we move through the sessions, we'll do it again, to check in to see what progress has been made and what they need to work on. Often, when one area improves, this can have a knock-on effect to other areas too.

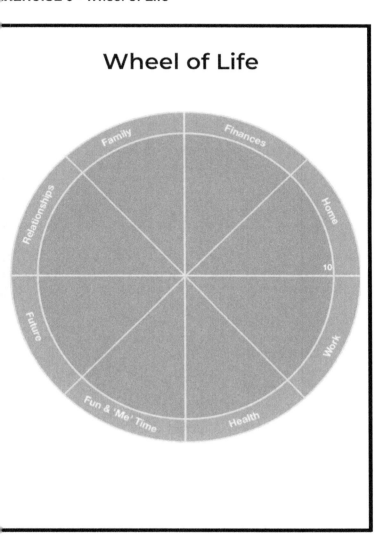

By doing this exercise, you'll raise your awareness around several areas of your life.

- You'll then be able to plan around those areas to make them more satisfying and balanced for you.

- A regular check-in with this exercise every so often can highlight useful patterns and help you learn more about yourself.

1. Taking each of the areas in the wheel separately, think about what success or satisfaction would feel like for each area.

2. Now rate your level of satisfaction within each area of your life by drawing a line across each segment. Place a value between 0 (very dissatisfied) and 10 (fully satisfied) against each area to show how satisfied you are currently with each category in their life. Don't think too much about it. Use the FIRST number that pops into your head, not the number you think it should be.

3. The new perimeter of the circle represents your Wheel of Life. How bumpy is your ride?

4. Now, looking at the wheel:

   - Are there any surprises for you?

   - How do you feel about your life as you look at your Wheel?

   - How do you *currently* spend time in these areas? How would you *like* to spend time in these areas?

   - What would need to happen to make them score of 10?

   - What would a score of 10 look like?

   - Which of these categories would you *most* like to improve?

   - How could you make space for these changes in your life?

- What help and support might you need from others to make changes and be more satisfied with your life?

- What change *can* you make first? And what change do you *want* to make first?

- If there was one key action you could take that would begin to bring everything into balance, what would it be?

5. Taking action - the final step. Choose the 3 areas you most want to work on.

EXERCISE 10 - Goal Setting

Goal Setting		
Where I am now	What do I need to do to get there	Where I want to be

So now you have three areas to work on, you can start by working out what you need to do to get where you want to be.

Your big 'Why"

First of all, you don't have to have a big goal. It could be something very simple to start with, such as going for a 10-minute walk

3 times a week.   But you do need a big "Why". A big enough reason to want to do achieve it. To want to go out for a 10 minute walk 3 times a week.

If you haven't got a big enough 'Why' you want to improve a particular area of your life, then you're unlikely to be motivated to do it.

So, for example, thinking that you want to improve your health but not thinking about why you want to do that simply won't work. Take a moment to think about *why* you want to do it. What does improving your health mean to you?

- Does it mean you'll stop smoking and be able to breathe more freely?
- Does it mean that you'll be able to run up the stairs instead of clambering up holding onto the rail?
- Does it mean that you'll have more energy to play with your children?
- Does it mean you'll be able to wear more stylish clothes?
- What does it mean for *you*?

And how will you know when you've achieved your goal?
- What will have changed?
- What might you be doing differently?
- How will you feel?
- What will you see?
- What might be going on around you?

What might stop you?
- What might get in the way of you achieving your goal?
- What help might you need to ensure that you pull through?
- Where can you find that help?

Setting future goals

So, what goals or outcomes do you want to achieve?   What are your top three?
Write them down.

In the goal setting chart above, for each goal make a note of where you are now and where you want to be. Then fill in the middle column of what you might need to help you get the outcome you want. What help might you need? Where can you find that? Do you need to learn any new skills? Will you need to make any changes?

CHAPTER 20

SUMMARY

Ending a relationship can be a painful, emotional experience. Not knowing what to do and how to cope can be challenging and overwhelming.

We hope this book has given you some ideas of how to think things through before you make your decision to divorce, insight into the divorce process itself, some practical tips on how to work with your emotions and plan for the future.

You should have a good understanding of the process, ideas of where to go for help and support, how to take care of yourself and look to the future.

Divorce isn't the end of the world, it's the end of your marriage. You might not think so just now, but there is life after divorce. Getting the right support, you need will help you get through it.

"The secret of change is to focus all of your energy not on fighting the old, but on building the new" -Socrates.

USEFUL LINKS

Divorce Coaching:
Margaret Yates margaret@margaretyates.co.uk
Divorce and Separation Coach
margaretyates.co.uk
https://www.linkedin.com/in/margaretyates1/

Legal Advice:
Farzana Naz fnaz@saracenssolicitors.co.uk
Family Solicitor
Saracens Solicitors
https://saracenssolicitors.co.uk/member/farzana-naz/

Domestic Violence Helpline
Refuge 0808 2000 247 (24hr)
https://www.nationaldahelpline.org.uk/en/Your-rights-and-options

www.gov.uk
How to divorce
Courts and Tribunals fees

Finances
Money Advice and Budgeting moneyadviceservice.org.uk
Debt Advice https://www.nationaldebtline.org

Mediation
Family Mediation Centre. https://www.fmcstaffs.co.uk/
Family Mediation Council https://www.familymediationcouncil.org.uk/
Start Mediation Ltd https://www.startmediation.co.uk/
National Family Mediation. https://www.nfm.org.uk/

Relaxation Techniques - Virtual and workshops
- Michael Burke Tai Chi https://taichimindbody.com
- Alessandro Ferrullo Qi Gong. https://flowinghealth.co.uk
- Sam Rao Yoga: Yoga https://www.patreon.com/samraoyoga

Parents
Gingerbread https://www.gingerbread.org.uk/
Families Need Fathers https://fnf.org.uk/
Only Dads https://www.onlydads.org/
Only Mums. https://www.onlymums.org/

Children
Voices in the Middle. https://www.voicesinthemiddle.com/
Divorce Is Not the End of the World https://www.amazon.co.uk/
Divorce-Not-End-World-Coping/dp/1582462410

Counselling
Relate. https://www.relate.org.uk/
Separation and Divorce Counselling. https://www.counselling-directory.org.uk/separation.html#whendocouplesdecidetodivorce

Printed in Great Britain
by Amazon

17213232R00068